Great Little Sweet Treats

Crafts From Your Kitchen

Great Little
Sweet Treats
Crafts From Your Kitchen

by Vanessa-Ann

Meredith® Press
Des Moines, Iowa

-♥ Michael ♥-

Write it on
your heart
that since the day
we were married,
every day is
the best day
of my life.

I love you.

Dear Reader,

Sweet surprises are always a delight to give friends and family or display as decor. All year long, gifts you make in the kitchen and present from the heart make celebrations and special occasions even nicer. In *Great Little Sweet Treats*, you'll find enchanting, delectable and decorative ways to say "Thank you," "Happy Birthday," "Congratulations" or simply "I love you".

Brought to you by Vanessa-Ann, *Great Little Sweet Treats* features a unique selection of food project designs. You'll find ideas for everything from old-fashioned hearts and flowers to contemporary cookie trees to lovable bears and ladybugs.

So whether you love spending time creating elaborate gifts from food or you are looking for quick-to-fix ideas, you'll find choices galore in *Great Little Sweet Treats*. All the projects are shown in full color and the helpful patterns and clear instructions make assembling these projects a pleasure.

We at Meredith® Press and Vanessa-Ann are dedicated to bringing you creative projects that meet your needs. We hope you'll enjoy making the projects in *Great Little Sweet Treats* and turn to our book whenever you need a special gift or celebration idea.

Sincerely,

Pat Van Note
Pat Van Note
Product Development Manager

ISBN: 0-696-02377-6
First Printing: 1992
Library of Congress Catalog number: 92-060551

Published by Meredith® Press

Distributed by Meredith® Corporation,
Des Moines, Iowa.

10987654321

Meredith[®] Press is an imprint of Meredith[®] Books

President, Book Group: Joseph J. Ward

Vice-President, Editorial Director: Elizabeth P. Rice

For Meredith[®] Press:

Product Development Manager: Patricia Van Note

Editorial Project Manager: Rosemary Hutchinson

Production Manager: Bill Rose

– ♥ –

The Vanessa~Ann Collection

Terrece Beesley and Jo Packham, Owners

Kathi Allred

Gloria Zirkel Baur

Sandra Durbin Chapman

Kristi Glissmeyer

Susan Jorgensen

Margaret Shields Marti

Barbara Milburn

Lisa Miles

Pamela Randall

Lynda Sessions Sorenson

Florence Stacey

Nancy Whitley

– ♥ –

Designers

Terrece Beesley

Kathy Burt

Holly Fuller

Tina Richards Herman

Sally Neill

Jo Packham

Lynda Sessions Sorenson

Florence Stacey

Cookies

Cakes

Candies

Cookies

Sun, Moon and Stars

2 cups packed brown sugar

1½ cups butter or margarine,
  softened

1 egg

4 cups all-purpose flour

2 teaspoons ground cinnamon

1 teaspoon ground nutmeg

½ teaspoon ground cloves

¼ teaspoon baking soda

Lightweight cardboard

In large mixing bowl, beat together sugar and butter. Add egg; beat until light and fluffy. In separate bowl, stir together dry ingredients. Add to beaten mixture; mix well. Cover and chill until firm, about 2 hours.

Preheat oven to 350 degrees. Using patterns on pages 12 and 13, cut shapes from cardboard. On floured surface, roll dough to ¼-inch thickness. Using the cardboard shapes, cut cookies from the dough with a small, sharp knife. Transfer to ungreased cookie sheet. Lightly draw faces on sun and moon cookies with a toothpick. Using scraps of dough, build eyebrows, noses, lips and mustache as shown in photo. For each star cookie; place 1 smaller star shape on 1 larger star shape as shown in photo. Bake for 10 to 15 minutes or until lightly browned.

Cool for 10 minutes before removing from cookie sheet. Remove to wire rack and cool completely. Makes about 3 dozen 6-inch cookies.

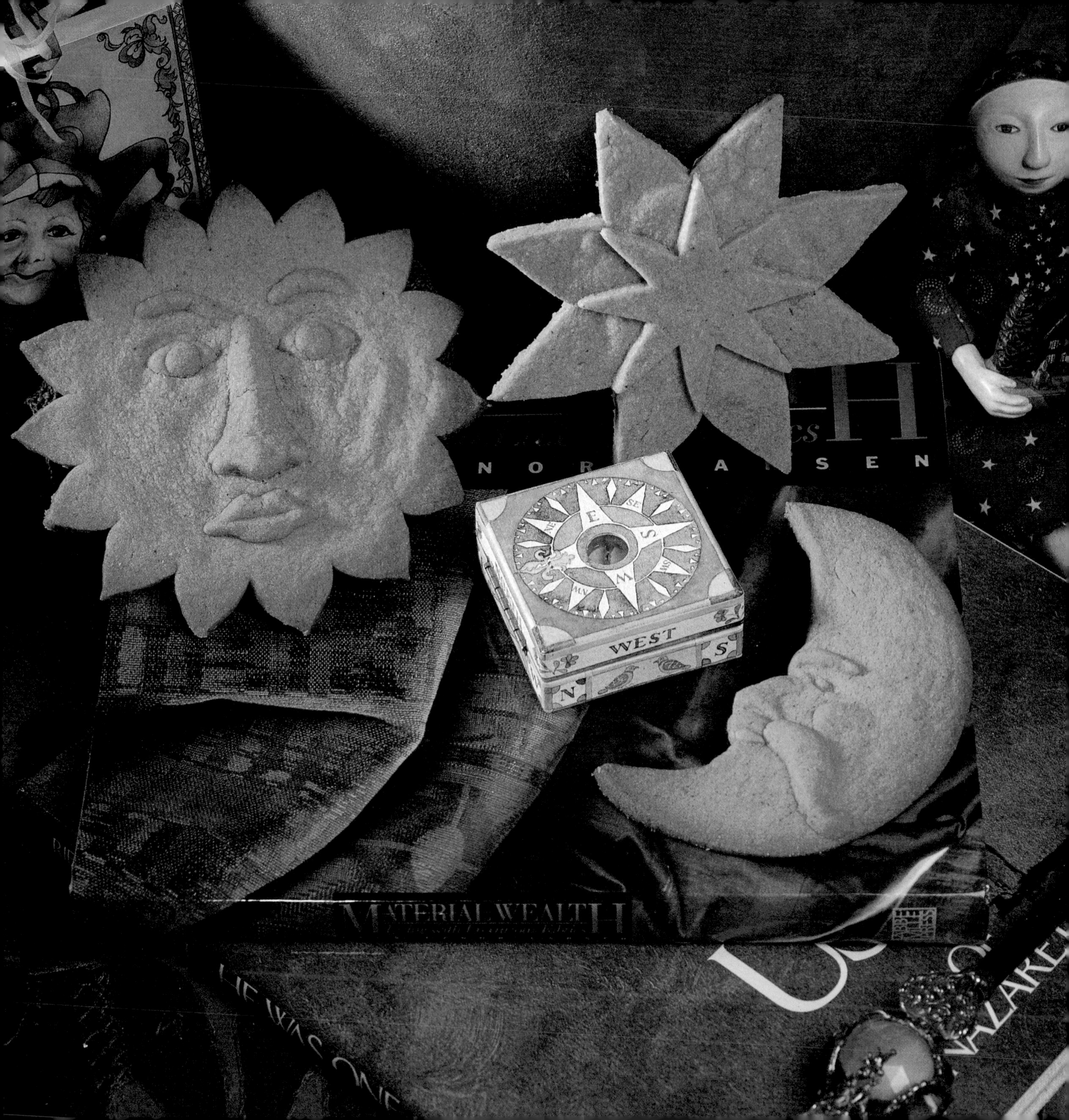
WEST
MATERIAL WEALTH

Sun, Moon and Stars

13

Party Perfect Pansies

½ **cup butter or margarine, softened**

½ **cup shortening**

1 **cup sifted powdered sugar**

1 **egg**

1½ **to 2 teaspoons lemon extract**

2½ **cups all-purpose flour**

½ **teaspoon salt**

Edible Decorator Paint; see page 18

¼**-inch flat paintbrush**

Liner paintbrush

In large mixing bowl, beat together butter and shortening. Gradually add sugar, beating until light and fluffy. Add egg and lemon extract; beat well. Combine flour and salt; stir into beaten mixture. Divide dough into thirds. Shape each third into a roll, about 1½ inches in diameter. Wrap each roll in plastic wrap and refrigerate for 2 to 3 hours.

Preheat oven to 375 degrees. Cut dough into ⅛-inch-thick slices. If dough cracks or crumbles while slicing or shaping, let stand at room temperature for 15 to 30 minutes before using. For each cookie, arrange 5 slices on an ungreased cookie sheet to resemble a pansy. The first 2 slices should overlap slightly. The second 2 should be side by side and overlapping the first 2 slices. The last slice should be centered between the third and fourth slices (Diagram 1). Press lightly in the center of the flower, making an indentation. Press in the edge of each slice to make flower petal appearance (Diagram 2). Bake for 7 to 8 minutes.

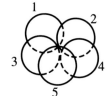
Diagram 1

Diagram 2

Prepare **Edible Decorator Paint** according to recipe. Use a light coat of watered-down paint for the base color, taking care not to get cookie too wet. Use a soft, clean, ¼-inch flat brush for base coat and shading. Use a liner brush for detail work. When dry, paint on shading and details, if desired. When painting the cookies, it is helpful to have pictures of real pansies to refer to. Return cookies to cookie sheet and bake for 2 minutes more to set the paint. Remove to rack and cool completely. Makes 2 dozen pansy-shaped cookies.

Happy Hamburger Days

20 chocolate sandwich-style cookies

Powdered Sugar Icing
2 tablespoons butter or margarine
3 tablespoons milk
1½ teaspoons vanilla
6 cups sifted powdered sugar

Green, pink, red and yellow paste food
   coloring

12 ounces vanilla wafers
Sesame seeds

Pull chocolate cookies apart and scrape off and discard the frosting. Divide **Powdered Sugar Icing** into 3 small bowls. Color icing with food coloring to resemble colors of lettuce, ketchup and mustard, using instructions on page 24 for coloring red icing. For each hamburger, spread green icing on the flat side of 1 vanilla wafer. Spread a thin layer of red icing on the flat side of a second vanilla wafer. Also add to the second wafer several spots of yellow icing. Place 1 chocolate cookie piece on top of the wafer with the red icing. Then place green-iced wafer, icing side down, on chocolate piece. Squeeze all 3 pieces together gently so that the icing extends slightly past the edges of the cookies. Brush water lightly onto rounded side of the top vanilla wafer and sprinkle with sesame seeds. Makes 3 dozen sandwich-style cookies.

Powdered Sugar Icing
In medium saucepan, heat butter and milk together until butter melts. Remove from heat and add vanilla. Gradually add powdered sugar to butter mixture until icing is thick; stir until smooth.

Love Letters

2 cups butter or margarine, softened

1 cup sugar

1 tablespoon water

1 tablespoon almond extract

5 cups all-purpose flour

Small (3½ x 6½-inch) paper
  envelope

Edible Decorator Paint

1 egg yolk

½ teaspoon water

Assorted colors of paste food coloring

Small, soft paintbrush

Powdered Sugar Icing; see page 16

In large mixing bowl, beat together butter and sugar. Add water and extract; mix well. Stir in flour until well combined. Cover and chill for 2 to 3 hours.

Preheat oven to 350 degrees. On floured surface, roll dough to a ¼-inch thickness. Using the envelope as a pattern, cut shapes in dough with a sharp knife. Reroll dough scraps. Cut out 1-inch squares of dough to resemble stamps. Transfer letters and stamps to ungreased cookie sheet with a spatula. Using a paintbrush, paint addresses, postmarks and stamps with **Edible Decorator Paint**. Allow each color of paint to dry thoroughly before painting with additional colors. Bake cookies for 25 to 30 minutes, removing stamps if they start to brown.

Cool slightly and remove from cookie sheet. Cool completely. Prepare **Powdered Sugar Icing** according to recipe. Use to attach stamps to letters. Makes 9 to 11 envelope-size cookies.

Edible Decorator Paint
Mix egg yolk with water. Divide mixture into several small cups. Add paste food coloring as desired. If needed, add additional water, 1 drop at a time, to make paint the consistency of ink. Use thin coats of **Edible Decorator Paint.** Allow each color to dry before proceeding with the next color. In recipes using opaque or pastel **Edible Decorator Paint**, add white, paste or liquid, food coloring. This improves opaqueness and removes much of the yellow color of the egg yolk. Food painted with **Edible Decorator Paint** should always be returned to the oven for a few minutes to set the paint and cook the egg yolk.

Rainbow Trout

¾ **cup sugar**

⅓ **cup shortening**

6 **tablespoons butter or margarine,**
  softened

1 **egg**

1 **tablespoon milk**

1 **teaspoon vanilla**

2 **cups all-purpose flour**

1½ **teaspoons baking powder**

¼ **teaspoon salt**

Lightweight cardboard

3 **ounces brightly colored hard candy**

In a large mixing bowl, beat together sugar, shortening and butter until fluffy. Add egg, milk and vanilla; beat well. In a small bowl, mix together dry ingredients. Add dry ingredients to beaten mixture; mix well. Cover bowl and chill dough for 2 to 3 hours.

Preheat oven to 375 degrees. Using the fish patterns on pages 22 and 23, cut shapes from cardboard. Cut out the interior designs. On a floured surface, roll dough out to an $1/8$-inch thickness. Place cardboard shapes on the dough and cut out cookies around outside edge only, using a small, sharp knife. Transfer the cookies to a cookie sheet covered with aluminum foil. Place the pattern over the cookie again and cut out the inside shapes, being careful not to cut foil; remove the dough pieces.

Crush the candies while still in wrappers, using a hammer or a meat tenderizer. Unwrap candies and place in small bowls, keeping different colors separate. Fill the holes in the cookies with desired colors of crushed candy, mounding slightly. Bake for 8 to 10 minutes. Cool on the cookie sheet for 15 minutes. Carefully peel the cookies off of the foil. Makes 1 dozen fish-shaped cookies.

Rainbow Trout

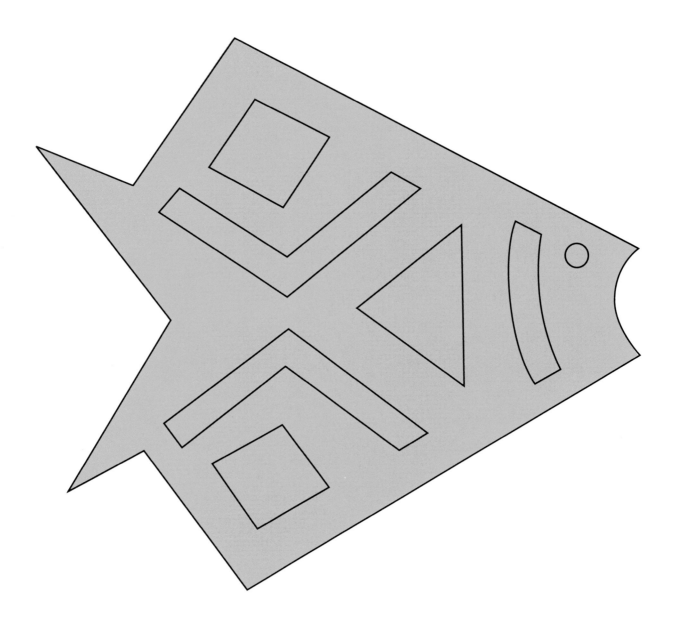

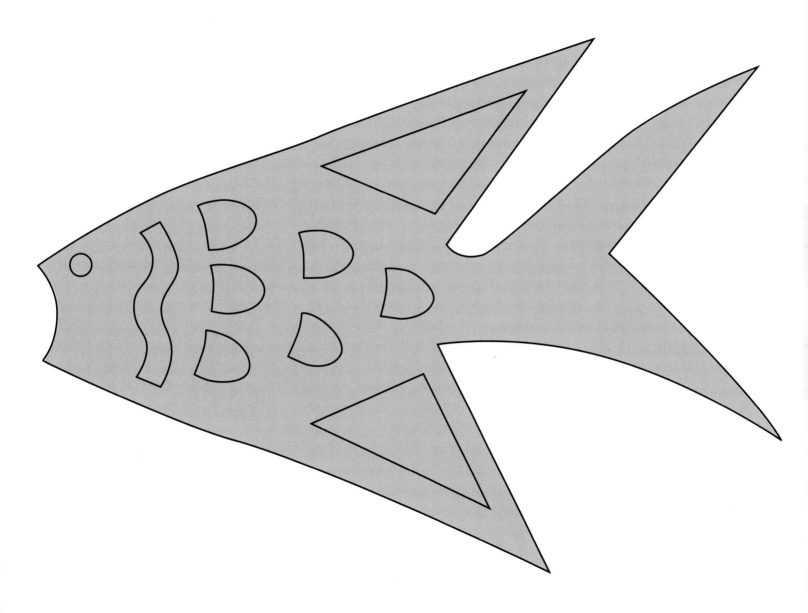

Party Pizzas

2 cups sugar

1¼ cups shortening

3 eggs

2 teaspoons vanilla

6 cups all-purpose flour

2 teaspoons salt

1 teaspoon baking powder

½ teaspoon baking soda

1 cup sour cream

Powdered Sugar Icing; see page 16

Red and pink paste food coloring

Yellow liquid food coloring

1 small bag grated coconut

3 (¾-ounce) red fruit leather snacks

6 ounces black licorice pieces

In large mixing bowl, beat together sugar and shortening. Add eggs, 1 at a time, beating well after each addition. Add vanilla. Beat until light in color. Sift dry ingredients together. Add sour cream alternately with dry ingredients to beaten mixture, beating well after each addition. Cover and chill dough overnight.

Preheat oven to 350 degrees. Pat dough into 5-inch rounds of ¼-inch thickness, adding more flour if needed. Bake on an ungreased cookie sheet for 10 minutes. Cool slightly and remove from the cookie sheet. Cool the cookies completely before decorating.

Prepare **Powdered Sugar Icing** according to recipe. To make red frosting, add pink food coloring to make a very deeply colored pink icing. Add just enough red food coloring to the pink icing to make it red. With this red icing, ice the tops of the cookies to resemble pizza sauce. In a small container with a tight fitting lid, put 5 or 6 drops of yellow food coloring. Add a third of the coconut to the container and cover; shake vigorously. Add more food coloring as needed until coconut is bright yellow. Sprinkle white and yellow coconut onto the iced cookies to resemble cheese. From fruit leather, cut out 1-inch circles. Place several circles onto each cookie to resemble pepperoni. Sprinkle licorice pieces onto cookies to resemble chopped olives. Makes 3 to 4 dozen pizza cookies.

America Celebrates

1 cup sugar

½ cup shortening

¼ cup butter or margarine,
  softened

2 eggs

1½ teaspoons vanilla

2½ cups all-purpose flour

½ teaspoon baking powder

½ teaspoon salt

Patriotic Frosting

2 tablespoons butter or margarine,
  softened

¼ cup milk

1 teaspoon vanilla

3 cups sifted powdered sugar

Red, pink, blue, green and white
  paste food coloring

½ to 1 teaspoon blueberry extract
  (optional)

½ to 1 teaspoon cherry extract
  (optional)

Decorative silver beads

White sprinkles

Red fruit leather

In large mixing bowl, mix together sugar, shortening, butter, eggs and vanilla; beat until creamy. Stir in flour, baking powder and salt; mix until well combined. Cover bowl and refrigerate for at least 1 hour.

Preheat oven to 400 degrees. On lightly floured surface, roll dough to an ⅛-inch thickness. Cut into desired shapes using cookie cutters or patterns on pages 28 and 29; cut from cardboard. Bake on ungreased cookie sheet for 6 to 8 minutes or until light brown. Cool completely.

Frost cookies as desired with **Patriotic Frosting**. Decorate cookies with beads, sprinkles and strips of red fruit leather. (Fruit leather can be cut into strips with scissors.) NOTE: Silver beads are for decoration only; remove before eating cookies. Makes 3 dozen cookies.

Patriotic Frosting

In medium mixing bowl, beat together butter, milk and vanilla. Add powdered sugar and beat until smooth. Add additional milk, 1 teaspoon at a time, if needed, to make frosting of spreading consistency. Divide frosting into 3 small bowls. Color 1 red, (using instructions on page 24), 1 blue and leave the last 1 white. To blue frosting, add blueberry extract, if desired. To red frosting, add cherry extract, if desired. Remove 1 tablespoon of frosting from the white frosting and color it green. White paste food coloring can be added to the remaining white frosting, if desired. Makes enough frosting to decorate 3 dozen cookies.

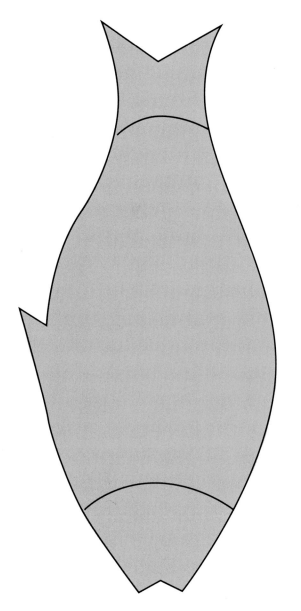

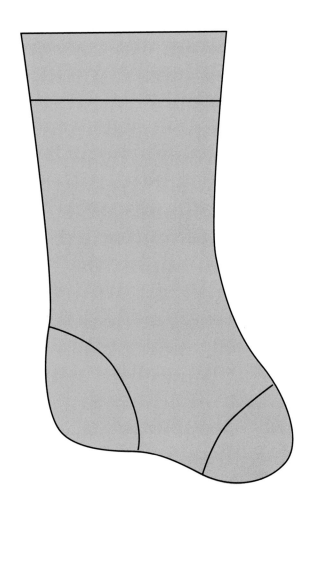

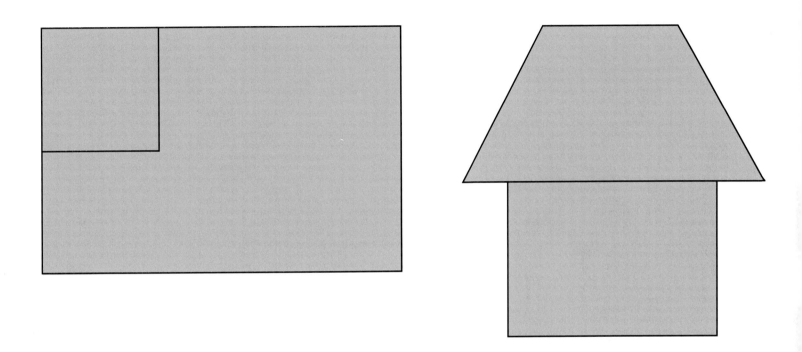

Bird House Cookie Jar

You will need one ½ x 9 x 24-inch, one ¾ x 18 x 48-inch and one 1 x 4 ½-inch **piece of pine** and a 3-inch piece of ½-inch-wide **dowel**. You will also need a **table saw**, **jig saw**, **drill** with ½-inch bit, **sandpaper**, **wood glue**, **manila folder**, **paint brushes**, **masking tape**, white, navy, light blue, red and green **acrylic paints** and **wood sealer**.

Cut 2 roof pieces 8 x 9 inches long from ½-inch pine. Bevel both 8-inch edges at 45-degree angles (Diagram 1). Cut 2 front/back pieces from ¾-inch pine (Diagram 2). In front piece, cut 2¼-inch-wide hole for opening. Drill ½-inch-wide hole at X on front piece for dowel. Cut 2 side pieces 5 x 6½-inches long from ¾-inch pine. Bevel top 5-inch edge at 45-degree angle (Diagram 3). Cut a 5 x 5¼-inch bottom piece from ¾-inch pine. Bevel 2 side pieces at an 81-degree angle (Diagram 4). Sand all pieces.

Glue and nail front and back pieces to base. Glue and nail side pieces to front and back and base, aligning top edges and bottom outside edges. Glue and insert dowel. Glue and nail roof pieces together. Center support on inside of roof; attach. Roof will be detachable lid.

Paint all, except roof, white, applying 2 coats if needed. Paint underside of roof red. Paint top of roof dark blue. Cut stencils for stars, tulip and stems from manila folder. Working from left at top edge of roof, mark 2 inches, 3½ inches, 5½ inches and 7 inches. Place masking tape on marks to create 2 areas ½ inch wide. Paint red between tape; allow to dry. Place tape in center of each red stripe. Paint light blue on both sides over red; allow to dry. Remove tape. Center star stencil vertically in remaining dark blue areas. Paint white stars, applying 2 coats if needed.

Mark parallel to and 1¾ inches above bottom of bird house. Place tape above line. Paint sides, back and front of house light blue below tape. Remove tape. On each side of bird house, mark placement for stems, beginning in center and about 2 inches on either side of center. Stencil green stem/leaves on marks. Add stem (but not leaves) between. Paint tulips and dowel red. Sponge paint edges of roof/lid light blue. Sponge paint bottom edge of bird house green.

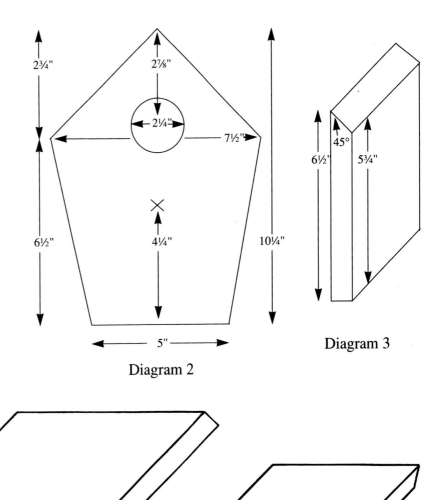

Diagram 2

Diagram 3

Diagram 1

Diagram 4

31

Nutty Little Owls

1 cup butter or margarine, softened

1 cup sugar

1 cup packed brown sugar

2 eggs

1 teaspoon vanilla

2 cups all-purpose flour

2 teaspoons baking soda

½ teaspoon salt

1 cup peanut butter or cashew butter

2 ounces unsweetened chocolate, melted

6 ounces semisweet chocolate pieces
30 cashews

In large mixing bowl, beat together butter, sugars, eggs and vanilla. Add flour, baking soda and salt to butter mixture; mix until well combined.

Separate half of the dough and place in a medium bowl. Add peanut butter and mix well. To the remaining dough, add melted chocolate; stir until well combined.

On a lightly floured surface, roll half of the light dough into a ¼-inch-thick rectangle on a 4½ x 12-inch piece of foil. Shape half of the brown dough into a 1½-inch-diameter log (about 12 inches long). Place at 1 short end of light rectangle. Using the foil for control, roll the rectangle of dough around the log. Repeat with the remaining doughs. Place the 2 rolls in the refrigerator to chill thoroughly for at least 4 hours.

Preheat oven to 350 degrees. Slice each roll into 24 slices ¼ inch thick. For each owl, place 2 slices next to each other on an ungreased cookie sheet and press slices together. Shape horns on the top edge of the top slice. Add chocolate pieces for the eyes and a whole cashew for the beak. Cut 2 slashes on each side of the bottom slice to resemble talons. Bake for about 10 minutes. Remove from cookie sheet; cool on wire rack. Makes 2 dozen owl-shaped cookies.

Honey Bears

2 cups honey

⅓ cup shortening, melted

2 eggs

½ cup milk

1 teaspoon vanilla

½ teaspoon salt

5 cups all-purpose flour

2 teaspoons baking powder

1½ teaspoons ground cinnamon

1 teaspoon baking soda

10 ounces miniature multi-colored
   candy-coated chocolate pieces

Preheat oven to 350 degrees. In large mixing bowl, combine honey and shortening. Add eggs, milk, vanilla and salt; beat well. Sift together flour, baking powder, cinnamon and baking soda. Add dry ingredients to honey mixture; beat well.

For each bear, roll a piece of dough into a 1½-inch ball for the body and a 1-inch ball for the head. Roll 6 balls ¼ inch in diameter for the ears, hands and feet. Roll a smaller piece of dough for the nose and then add a tiny piece of dough to the tip of the nose. Form bears directly on a greased cookie sheet. Place the pieces of each bear so that they are slightly touching each other and the bears are 2 inches apart. With the palm of your hand, gently press down on each bear so that the pieces will join to each other, being careful not to completely flatten the bears. Insert colored candy pieces into bears for the eyes and belly button. Bake for 12 minutes; do not overbake. Cool slightly; remove from cookie sheet to wire rack. Makes 3 to 4 dozen.

Honey Bear Basket

You will need a small **stuffed bear**, a 7-inch-wide **basket** with a lid, 2 wooden **buckets** 2 inches wide, a **hot glue gun**, two or three 12-inch **glue sticks**, **paintbrushes** and **Great Glass staining medium** in yellow and brown.

Glue bear and buckets to basket lid. Melt hot glue in the upright bucket until full. Melt glue in overturned bucket and onto basket top and bear. Mix paint to color desired. Paint surface of glue.

repairs old
He must work at
job every day of the
so he has enough
toys for all the children
at Christmas time.
Santa made a special
Kitty Cucumber
TEDDY
Old Fashioned
CHRISTMAS BELLS
B
SANTA=CLAUS
KRISS KRINGLE
PICTURE
SANTA CLAUS
B

Fruits of Summer

1 cup butter or margarine, softened

1 cup sugar

2 eggs

¼ cup milk

½ teaspoon vanilla

3½ cups all-purpose flour

Assorted fruit-flavored extracts

Assorted colors of paste food coloring

Buttercream Filling

1 cup sifted powdered sugar

⅓ cup butter or margarine, softened

1 teaspoon vanilla

Tinted Sugars

Sugar

Assorted colors of paste food coloring

Small, soft paintbrush

Whole cloves

Black shoestring licorice

Preheat oven to 350 degrees. In a large mixing bowl, cream butter. Gradually add sugar, beating until light and fluffy. Add eggs, milk and vanilla; beat well. Add flour, beating well. Divide dough into portions depending on fruits desired. Add appropriate extract and food coloring to each portion. For all fruits, except grapes and cherries, shape dough into 1-inch balls and place 2 inches apart on ungreased cookie sheet. For grapes, make ¼-inch balls of dough; for cherries, make ½-inch balls. Bake for 10 minutes, or until bottoms are light brown. Cool on wire racks.

To form the fruit, spread a little **Buttercream Filling** on flat side of a cookie. Place the flat side of a second cookie of the same size and color on filling, pressing together gently. Repeat for all.

Using a paintbrush, coat each cookie lightly with water. Roll cookies in appropriate color of **Tinted Sugars**. Let cookies stand 15 minutes. To make stems, carefully press a whole clove in the seam at the top of each cookie, except for grapes and cherries. To make stems for cherries, carefully make a small hole in seam at top with a toothpick and insert a 1-inch piece of licorice. Leave grapes without stems. Makes 1 dozen fruit-shaped cookies.

Buttercream Filling
In small mixing bowl, cream powdered sugar and butter, beating until light and fluffy. Add vanilla; beat well.

Tinted Sugars
For each color desired, add small amount of desired paste food coloring to ⅓ cup sugar. Mix together thoroughly.

Knotted-Corner Tray

You will need one 18-inch-square **cotton napkin** and a shallow square **wood box or** small square **cake pan**. Knot 2 corners of napkin loosely. Place napkin, right side up, in the box or pan and place knots at corners. Knot remaining 2 corners loosely. Adjust the knots on all 4 corners so the napkin will fit snugly at the corners.

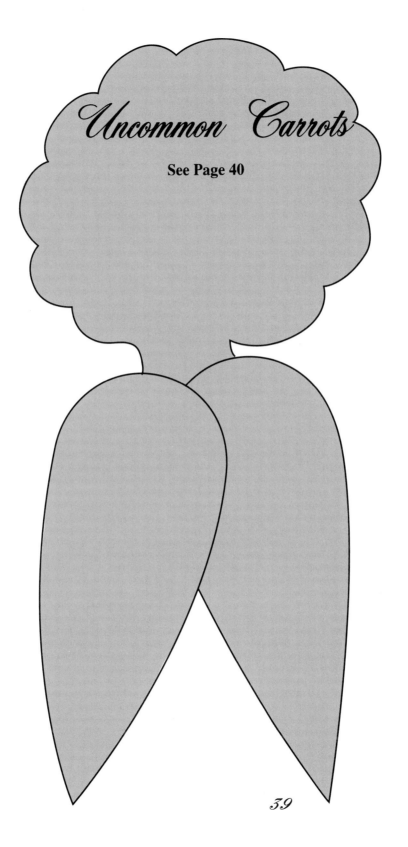

Uncommon Carrots

See Page 40

Uncommon Carrots

1 cup sugar

½ cup shortening

¼ cup butter or margarine, softened

2 eggs

1½ teaspoons vanilla

2½ cups all-purpose flour

½ teaspoon baking powder

½ teaspoon salt

½ teaspoon ground cinnamon

¼ teaspoon ground allspice

Lightweight cardboard

Orange candy coating pieces

Small, soft paintbrush

Red paste food coloring

Green candy coating pieces

Green liquid food coloring

Shredded coconut

In large mixing bowl, mix together sugar, shortening, butter, eggs and vanilla; beat until creamy. Stir in flour, baking powder, salt and spices; mix until well combined. Cover bowl and refrigerate for at least 1 hour.

Preheat oven to 400 degrees. Using carrot pattern on page 39, cut shapes from cardboard. On lightly floured surface, roll dough to an ⅛-inch thickness. Lay cardboard shapes on dough and cut out cookies with a sharp knife. Place cookie dough shapes on a greased cookie sheet. Bake for 6 to 8 minutes or until light brown. Cool slightly on pan. Transfer to wire rack and cool completely before decorating.

In a double boiler, melt the orange candy coating pieces. With a paintbrush, paint the light orange area on the carrot cookies. Add a little red paste food coloring to the remaining orange candy coating. Outline and add the small lines to the carrots with the darker orange candy coating. Melt the green candy coating pieces and paint the leaves.

In a small container with a tight fitting lid, put 6 to 10 drops of green liquid food coloring. Add the coconut; shake vigorously. Add more food coloring as needed, until desired color is reached. Decorate the leaves of the carrots with the coconut. Makes 2 dozen carrot-shaped cookies.

Autumn Leaves

1½ cups sugar

1 cup butter or margarine

3 eggs

4 cups all-purpose flour

1½ teaspoons baking powder

1½ teaspoons baking soda

½ teaspoon salt

⅔ cup sour cream

¼ cup milk

1 teaspoon vanilla

Lightweight cardboard

Edible Decorator Paint; see page 18

½ cup semisweet chocolate pieces

Baking parchment

Water

2 cups sifted powdered sugar

In large mixing bowl, beat together sugar and butter. Add eggs; beat well. In smaller bowl, combine dry ingredients. Combine sour cream, milk and vanilla. Add dry ingredients and milk mixture alternately to sugar mixture, beating after each addition. Cover and chill overnight or for at least 3 hours.

Preheat oven to 350 degrees. Using pattern on page 45, cut shapes from cardboard. On floured surface, roll dough to ¼-inch thickness. Lay the cardboard shapes on the dough and cut out cookies. Transfer to an ungreased cookie sheet. Prepare 3 or 4 colors of **Edible Decorator Paint** according to recipe. With pastry brush, lightly paint leaves, blending colors. Bake for 8 to 10 minutes or until edges begin to brown. Cool for 1 minute. Remove to wire rack. Cool.

For chocolate veins; in a microwave-safe bowl, melt chocolate pieces on HIGH power for 1 to 2 minutes, stirring once or twice. Make a parchment decorating cone. (See **General Instructions** on page 164 for making parchment cone.) Fill cone with melted chocolate, folding down top to seal cone. Cut a very small hole in tip of cone and gently squeeze a thin line of chocolate onto cookies to create leaf veins. Dry completely. Glaze.

To glaze cookies add water to powdered sugar to make a fairly liquid consistency. (Glaze should be transparent, not opaque.) Place several cookies at a time on a wire rack and place rack over pan to catch excess glaze. Pour glaze over cookies, covering each completely. Collect excess glaze and repeat process with remaining cookies. Dry completely. Makes 5 dozen leaf cookies.

Painted Leaf Box

You will need one $3^1/_2$-inch-deep 9-inch-wide **oval wood box** with lid, small and medium red **leaves**, 1 cup **glycerin**, **tacky glue**, Plaid Enterprise's **Treasure Crystal Cote**, and rust, light brown, green, purple and burgundy **acrylic paints**, bronze **metallic paint** and assorted sizes of **paintbrushes**.

Mix the glycerin with 1 cup of water and soak leaves in solution for 2 to 3 weeks. Paint all surfaces of wood box with rust paint. Glue leaves to sides of box and on 1 end of lid; see photo. Coat outside surfaces with Treasure Crystal Cote; allow to dry thoroughly. Using remaining colors of acrylic paints, highlight the portions of the box sides and lid that show and small parts of the leaves. Apply second coat of Treasure Crystal Cote; allow to dry. Paint center of some leaves with metallic paint, using brush or finger.

Autumn Leaves

Snow Buddies

Mold or cut small hearts and stars from **Play Clay.** With a toothpick, make holes in the shapes to be strung later. Allow all the **Play Clay** pieces to dry.

In a large mixing bowl, cream together sugars, butter and shortening until very light and fluffy. Add eggs, 1 at a time, beating well after each addition. Beat in the milk and vanilla. Sift together the dry ingredients. Add to shortening mixture; beat well. Cover and chill for 1 hour or until dough is easy to handle.

Preheat oven to 400 degrees. Roll dough to a ¼-inch thickness. Cut out with a snowman-shaped cookie cutter. Place on a greased cookie sheet. Bake for 8 to 10 minutes or until cookies just begin to brown. Cool for 1 minute on cookie sheet. While cookies are warm, use the handle of the paintbrush to make 5 indentations to resemble buttons, 5 indentations to resemble a smile, and 2 indentations to resemble eyes in each snowman. Make 1 hole in the top of each snowman's head and 1 hole in either 1 or 2 hands. Using food coloring, lightly paint the inside of the indentations black. With red food coloring, lightly redden each snowman's cheeks. Prepare dusty orange-colored **Little Gourmet Clay** according to recipe. For each snowman, mold a small carrot-shaped nose. Attach nose with corn syrup.

String the 2 **Play Clay** hearts and 1 star on floss and attach to holes in 2 hands or tie a star to a cinnamon stick and attach the cinnamon stick to the hole in 1 hand. Thread floss through hole in top of each snowman's head and tie a loop. NOTE: The stars,

Play Clay
2 cups baking soda
1¼ cups water
1 cup cornstarch
Assorted colors of paste food coloring

1¼ cups sugar
¼ cup packed brown sugar
⅓ cup butter or margarine, softened
⅓ cup shortening
2 eggs
4 teaspoons milk
1 teaspoon vanilla
3 cups all-purpose flour
2 teaspoons baking powder
½ teaspoon salt
¼ teaspoon ground nutmeg

Black and red paste food coloring
Little Gourmet Clay; see page 134
Corn syrup

Light brown embroidery floss
Cinnamon sticks

hearts, embroidery floss and cinnamon sticks are for decoration only; remove before eating cookies. Noses can also be made with appropriate color **Play Clay** and glued onto snowmen. The entire cookie would then be for decoration only. Makes about 3 dozen 2½-inch snowman-shaped cookies.

Play Clay
In a medium-size heavy saucepan, combine all ingredients and mix until smooth. Boil for 1 minute, stirring constantly, until the mixture is the consistency of mashed potatoes. Spoon the clay into a bowl. Cover the bowl with a damp cloth and let cool completely.

When cool, divide clay into batches for desired number of colors. Knead desired color of paste food coloring into each batch of clay. Combine colors to yield color variations. Mold or cut clay into desired shapes. Let dry for 24 to 48 hours. Unused dough can be kept in a plastic bag for several days.

Pie Dough Cookies

See Page 50

Pie Dough Cookies

2 cups sifted all-purpose flour
1¼ teaspoons salt
⅔ cup shortening
4 tablespoons water

Lightweight cardboard

Sugar
½ teaspoon ground cinnamon
Yellow liquid food coloring
Green liquid food coloring

Preheat oven to 400 degrees. In a large mixing bowl, mix together flour and salt. Cut in the shortening, until it is the size of small peas. Sprinkle with water. Gather the dough together and press into a ball.

Using the patterns on page 49, cut shapes from cardboard. On a floured surface, roll dough out to a ¼-inch thickness. Lay cardboard shapes on dough and cut out cookies with a sharp knife. Place cookie dough shapes on an ungreased cookie sheet. Mix ¼ cup sugar and cinnamon in a small bowl. In a small bowl, mix a small amount of sugar with a few drops of yellow food coloring and in another small bowl mix another small amount of sugar with a few drops of green food coloring. Sprinkle cookies with desired-color sugar. Bake for 3 to 5 minutes or until golden. Remove to wire rack and cool. Makes 4 dozen shaped cookies.

A Victorian Keepsake

1 cup sugar

1 cup dark molasses

½ cup shortening

½ cup water

4½ cups all-purpose flour

1½ teaspoons salt

1½ teaspoons ground ginger

½ teaspoon ground cloves

½ teaspoon ground nutmeg

¼ teaspoon ground allspice

Cream Cheese Icing

3 ounces cream cheese, softened

1 tablespoon butter or margarine, softened

1 teaspoon vanilla

2½ cups sifted powdered sugar

Little Gourmet Clay; see page 134

In large mixing bowl, stir together sugar, molasses, shortening and water. Mix in dry ingredients. Cover and chill for 3 hours.

Preheat oven to 375 degrees. On well-floured surface, roll dough to a ¼-inch thickness. Cut with heart-shaped cookie cutter. Place 1½ inches apart on ungreased cookie sheet. Bake for 10 to 12 minutes. Cool for 2 minutes before removing from the cookie sheet to a wire rack. Cool completely.

Spread **Cream Cheese Icing** on flat side of half of the cookies. Top with remaining cookies, rounded side up.

Prepare pink and green **Little Gourmet Clay** according to recipe. Mold roses and leaves; see page 134. Use dots of icing to attach roses and leaves to the top of the cookies. Toothpicks are helpful for moving small pieces. Makes 2 dozen sandwich-style cookies.

Cream Cheese Icing
In small mixing bowl, beat together cream cheese, butter, and vanilla. Add powdered sugar gradually; mix until smooth. Add more powdered sugar, if needed.

Velvet Heart Box

You will need 1 red velvet **heart-shaped candy box**, 1 cluster of **flowers**, 1 medium-sized **silk rose and bud**, 1 small **butterfly**, $1^1/_2$ yards of 1-inch-wide red wired **ribbon**, red, pink, dark green, lavender, purple, cream, light blue and dark blue **acrylic paints**, **gold metallic paint**, 2 sizes of small **paintbrushes** and a **hot glue gun and glue**.

Paint the outside of the bottom of the candy box gold. Paint the inside of both the top and bottom red. Once dry, paint the inside of both top and bottom with light coat of gold. Paint both sides of red ribbon with a light coat of gold. Fold ribbon into 3-inch-deep loops and glue to upper left of box top.

Separate and paint flowers, roses and butterflies as desired, using a variety of colors and painting both sides. Once dry, brush them lightly with gold. Reassemble bunches of flowers and roses and glue them to center of ribbon. Add butterflies.

Spring Showers

See Page 56

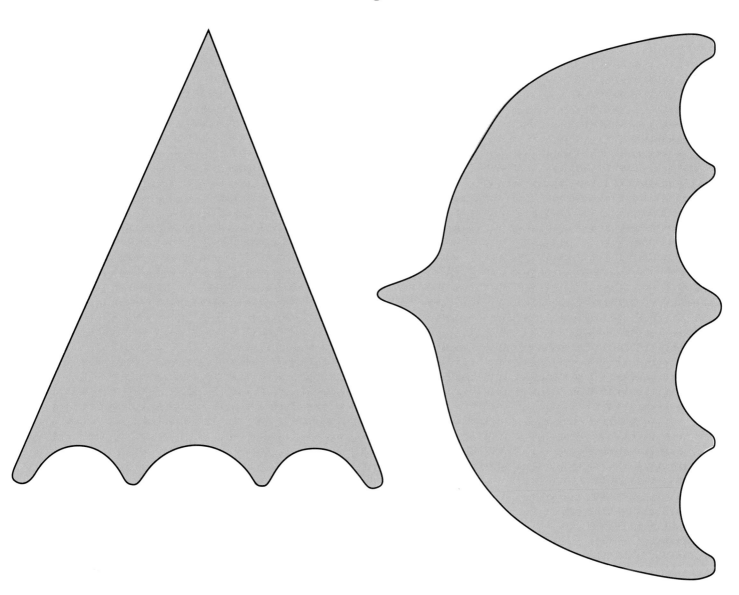

Spring Showers

¾ cup sifted powdered sugar

½ cup butter or margarine, softened

1 egg

1 teaspoon vanilla

1½ cups all-purpose flour

¼ cup unsweetened cocoa

½ teaspoon baking soda

½ teaspoon cream of tartar

Lightweight cardboard

24 craft sticks

Buttercream Frosting; see page 122

Blue, brown, yellow, green and violet
  paste food coloring

12 candy canes

12 candy sticks

Decorator bag

No. 3 writing tip

Decorative silver beads

Small round red cinnamon candies

In a large mixing bowl, mix together powdered sugar and butter. Stir in egg and vanilla; mix well. Add dry ingredients; stir until well combined. Cover bowl and refrigerate dough for 2 to 3 hours or until chilled.

Preheat oven to 375 degrees. Using the umbrella patterns on page 55, cut shapes from cardboard. On a floured surface, roll dough out to a ¼-inch thickness. Place cardboard shapes on cookie dough and cut out cookies with a sharp knife. Place cookies on an ungreased cookie sheet. Using 2 craft sticks per cookie, stack sticks and place under cookie where umbrella handle would go. The sticks will help the cookies bend slightly as they bake. Bake for 8 to 10 minutes or until set. Cool cookies for 1 minute; transfer to a wire rack and cool completely. Reuse craft sticks for next batch.

Prepare **Buttercream Frosting** according to recipe. Divide into 6 even portions and add paste food coloring to make desired colors, leaving 1 portion untinted. Frost ends of candy canes and candy sticks and attach to back of cookies as handles. Frost cookies with different colored frosting; see photo. Fill decorating bag with contrasting colors and No. 3 writing tip, add trims, dots and lines; see photo. Place beads and red candies as desired. NOTE: Silver beads are for decoration only; remove before eating the cookies. Makes 2 dozen umbrella-shaped cookies.

Tiny Tacos

12 fortune cookies

½ cup miniature semisweet
   chocolate pieces

2 tablespoons corn syrup

¼ cup green candy coating pieces

Yellow liquid food coloring

¼ cup grated coconut

10 small red gumdrops

Bring a medium saucepan of water to boiling and cover the top with a wire rack to let steam through. Place 1 or 2 fortune cookies, side down, on the rack and cover with the saucepan lid. Steam cookies for about 2 minutes. Turn cookies on to other side and steam, covered, another 1 or 2 minutes until soft. Place cookies on rounded edge and steam, covered, until flat. After the cookies flatten and while they are still soft, take them off the rack and fold them over the handle of a butter knife to make a taco shell shape. Hold until cool. Repeat with remaining cookies.

In a small bowl, combine chocolate pieces with corn syrup to hold pieces together. Set aside. In another bowl, grate the green candy coating. In a small container with a tight-fitting lid, put 2 or 3 drops of yellow food coloring and add the coconut. Cover and shake vigorously. Add more food coloring as needed until coconut is bright yellow. Cut the gum drops into small pieces.

Assemble the cookies the same way you would a taco. Place a small amount of the chocolate pieces mixture in the bottom of each cookie to resemble meat. Next add the green grated candy coating to resemble lettuce. Add some coconut to resemble cheese. Finally, top each cookie with a few pieces of the gum drops to resemble tomatoes. Makes 1 dozen taco-shaped cookies.

Button, Button...

½ **cup sugar**

½ **cup butter or margarine, softened**

1 egg

1 tablespoon milk

1 teaspoon vanilla

1¼ cups all-purpose flour

1 teaspoon cream of tartar

½ **teaspoon baking soda**

¼ **teaspoon salt**

½ **cup raspberry jelly**

Small, soft paintbrush

Edible Decorator Paint; see page 18

Blue, green, yellow and red paste food coloring

Powdered Sugar Icing; see page 16

Decorating bag

No. 3 writing tip

In a large mixing bowl, beat sugar and butter until light and fluffy. Add egg, milk and vanilla; mix well. Add dry ingredients; mix until well combined. Cover bowl and refrigerate dough for 3 hours or until firm.

Preheat oven to 350 degrees. Use only a third of the dough at a time; keep the remaining dough refrigerated. On a floured surface, roll dough out to a ⅓-inch thickness. Using a 12-ounce tumbler, cut out cookies. Place half the cookies on an ungreased cookie sheet. Put ½ teaspoon of raspberry jelly on each cookie. Top with remaining cookies. Using an 8-ounce tumbler, make indention to seal cookies. With the handle of the paintbrush, poke 4 holes in each cookie to resemble a button.

Prepare **Edible Decorator Paint** according to recipe, making desired colors. Using a paintbrush, paint cookies as desired; see photo. Bake for 3 to 5 minutes or until edges are lightly browned. Cool for 1 minute. Remove to wire racks and cool completely.

Prepare **Powdered Sugar Icing** according to recipe. Tint some green and a small portion of yellow. Tint another portion with the red paste food coloring to make a pink color. Using decorating bag and a No. 3 writing tip, decorate some of the button tarts as shown; see photo. Makes 3 dozen sandwich-style cookies.

Cinnamon Ornaments

In a medium mixing bowl, stir together cinnamon, glue and enough water to make a clay the consistency of cookie dough. Cover bowl and refrigerate the clay for 2 hours.

Working on a surface that has been sprinkled with cinnamon, knead clay until it is smooth. For garland shapes, roll the clay to a ¼-inch thickness. Cut 12 shapes into the clay with heart- and star-shaped cookie cutters. Lay shapes on waxed paper.

For angels, use the angel patterns on pages 66 and 67 to cut shapes from cardboard. With the cardboard shapes, cut angels from the clay with a small, sharp knife. Lay the angels on waxed paper to dry.

Dry at room temperature and turn shapes and angels over twice a day for 4 days or put on a cookie sheet and bake in a 200-degree oven for 2 hours, turning every half hour until all shapes are dry.

For each heart, use 10 pieces of 6- to 10-inch-long gold beading wire. Twist the wires together about 2 inches at 1 end. Position twisted wire to back of heart with untwisted lengths at bottom. Bring individual wire strands to the front and fan out evenly at the bottom. String beads onto wire, 1 wire at a time; see photo. When beading is complete, gather wires to a point at top of heart. Twist remaining wires together, make a small loop, and wrap wire tightly around twisted wire from the back until secure. Cut off extra wire.

1 cup ground cinnamon
¼ cup white glue
¾ to 1 cup water

Silver and gold beading wire
Assorted beads
Silver ribbon

Lightweight cardboard

Watercolor paper
Colored pencils
Craft glue
Assorted beads
Small pieces of lace
Yellow or white yarn
Metallic cording

For each star, use 12 pieces of 6- to 10-inch-long silver wire. Twist wires together about 2 inches at 1 end and position twisted wire in back of star with untwisted lengths at bottom. Bring wires to front and string bead onto each wire separately; see photo. Divide wires into groups of 4, wrapping 1 group over the top left corner of the star, the second group over the point and the last group over the top right corner. Twist all wires together in back, making a loop at the top and securing tightly. When all shapes have been beaded, string silver ribbon through wire loops, tying a knot at each loop to complete garland. Makes 12 shapes.

For each angel, use the face patterns to cut faces from watercolor paper. Draw details with colored pencils. Glue to the angel shapes with craft glue. Using craft glue to attach beads and lace, decorate the angels as desired; see photo. Attach yarn for hair. Make a loop with the metallic cording for hanging and glue to the back of the angel. Makes 6 ornaments.

NOTE: These ornaments are for decoration only, and neither the clay nor the finished ornaments are edible.

Cinnamon Ornaments

Cinnamon Ornaments

Star Cookie Tree

See Page 70

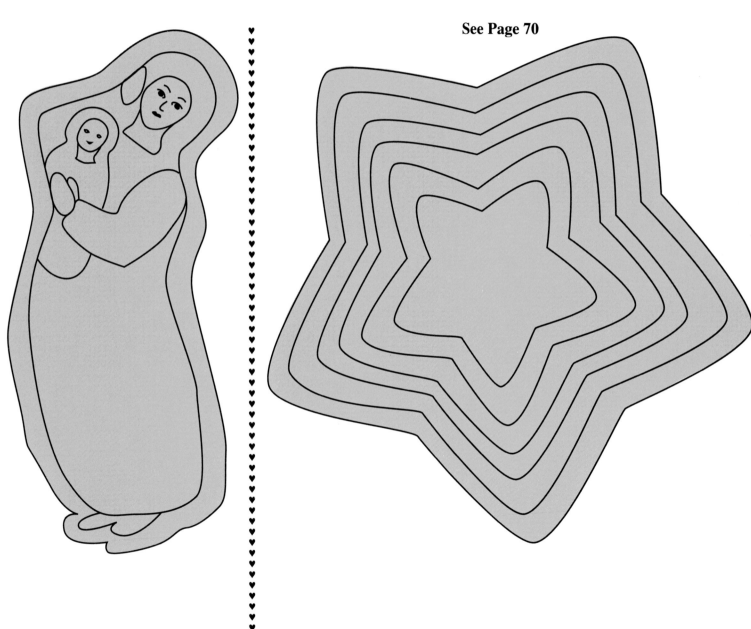

Oh, Christmas Trees

Sugar Cookie Tree

Cut out cardboard circle to make base of tree in size desired. Using glue gun, attach leaf-shaped cookies to lay flat around base. Add as many more layers of cookies as desired in the same manner. Toward the top, add small pieces of broken cookies in center, then a layer of whole cookies around the pieces; this will cause cookies to slant down to make tree shape. Repeat for 2 more layers. Glue star-shaped cookie at top. String miniature ornaments around tree, securing ends with glue at desired points. NOTE: This cookie tree is not edible.

Heavy cardboard

Hot glue gun

Glue sticks

4 dozen purchased leaf-shaped sugar cookies with colored sprinkles

1 purchased star-shaped sugar cookie with colored sprinkles

1 strand miniature tree ornaments

Gingerbread Men Tree

Lay gingerbread-men-shaped cookies on paper in a triangle shape; see photo. Trace around cookies for pattern. Using cardboard, cut 3 triangle shapes, making the shapes slightly smaller than the pattern. Glue cookies onto the cardboard with glue gun. After each triangle is covered with cookies, stand sections up and glue sides to form tree. Glue chocolate pieces onto cardboard to fill open spaces between cookies.

Thread 4 bells onto each of 3 equal lengths of red ribbon. Glue 1 end of each ribbon to treetop and bells at desired points along each seam of the tree. To make star, string red and green beads alternately onto wire. Leave bare wire at both ends and twist closed. Shape wire into a star. Glue each remaining bell to 2 star points. Glue star to treetop. NOTE: This tree is not edible.

4 dozen purchased gingerbread-men-shaped cookies

Heavy cardboard

Hot glue gun

Glue sticks

1 small bag red and green candy-coated chocolate pieces

14 small jingle bells

Red curling ribbon

15 small red bugle beads

15 small green bugle beads

1 (6-inch) piece of thin wire

1½ cups butter or margarine,
   softened

½ cup sugar

2 to 3 teaspoons eggnog extract

4 cups all-purpose flour

Lightweight cardboard or
   6 star cookie cutters in graduated
   sizes

Decorators' Buttercream Frosting

3½ cups sifted powdered sugar

½ cup white shortening

⅓ cup milk or water

1 teaspoon vanilla

¼ teaspoon salt

Star Cookie Tree

Preheat oven to 350 degrees. In large mixing bowl, mix together butter, sugar and extract. Work flour in with hands. If dough is crumbly, add an additional 1 to 2 tablespoons softened butter.

On a lightly floured surface, roll dough to a ½-inch thickness. Using pattern on page 67, cut star shapes from cardboard. Cut 2 of each size except for the smallest size. Cut 1 of the smallest size star for the treetop. Bake on an ungreased cookie sheet for about 15 to 20 minutes; avoid overbaking smaller cookies. Immediately remove from cookie sheet; let cool on wire rack.

Using ½ to 1 teaspoon of **Decorators' Buttercream Frosting** between cookies, stack stars beginning with the 2 largest and building up to the 2 smallest stars at top. Alternate the points of the stars. With a small amount of frosting, attach the extra small star upright at the top of tree. Add small mounds of frosting to tips of each star to resemble snow. Makes 1 star cookie tree.

Decorators' Buttercream Frosting
In a large mixing bowl, combine all ingredients, beating with a mixer at low speed until mixed well. Beat at high speed for 2 to 4 minutes until light and fluffy. Makes enough frosting for 1 star cookie tree.

Advent Calendar

You will need one 6-inch-wide piece of round ¾-inch **pine** for base, 1 yard of ⅛-inch-wide **wicker reed**, twelve ½-inch-wide white **wood beads**, twelve ½-inch-wide natural **wood beads**, one 1-inch-wide natural **wood heart**, **drill** with ⅛-inch bit and white craft **glue**.

Mark opposite edges of wood base and drill holes ½ inch deep at marks. Also drill hole through center of heart. Cut a 27-inch piece of reed. Glue 1 end into 1 hole. Thread reed through beads, alternating colors and ending with heart. Glue second end of reed into second hole. On December 1, place all beads on the end of the reed with the heart and move 1 bead a day until Christmas.

Lace-Like Hearts

In medium mixing bowl, beat together sugar and butter. Add egg and vanilla; beat well. Mix together dry ingredients. Add dry ingredients alternately with milk to butter mixture, beating well after each addition. Cover and chill for 2 to 3 hours.

Preheat oven to 325 degrees. Sift a layer of unsweetened cocoa onto a flat surface. Roll dough out to a ¼-inch thickness. Cut out cookies with heart-shaped cookie cutter. Place cookies on ungreased cookie sheet. Bake for 10 minutes. Cool slightly and remove from cookie sheet. When cool, spread **Almond Filling** on flat side of half of the cookies. Top with remaining cookies, rounded side up.

To stencil cookies, place cookies in center of a plate. Position lace or doily over cookie as desired. Sift powdered sugar onto cookie. Tap plate gently on counter to force sugar through holes in lace or doily. Carefully remove lace or doily, straight up.

To decorate cookies with beads, mix a small amount of powdered sugar and water to consistency of glue. Place small dots of icing on cookie and place beads on top of dots. NOTE: Silver beads are for decoration only; remove before eating the cookies. Makes 1½ dozen sandwich-style cookies.

Almond Filling
In small mixing bowl, combine sugar, butter, milk and extract. Stir until smooth and creamy. Tint with food coloring.

1 cup sugar

¾ cup butter or margarine, softened

1 egg

1 teaspoon vanilla

2¼ cups all-purpose flour

¾ cup unsweetened cocoa

1 teaspoon baking powder

½ teaspoon salt

½ teaspoon baking soda

¼ cup milk

Almond Filling

1½ cups sifted powdered sugar

3 tablespoons butter or margarine, softened

1 tablespoon milk

1 teaspoon almond extract

Peach paste food coloring

Small pieces of lace with porous design or paper doilies

Powdered sugar

Decorative silver beads

Victorian Box

You will need 1 round brown **papier mache box** with a lid; 4 or 5 assorted **fabric, crocheted or lace doilies; thread** to match; miscellaneous **beads, buttons, shells or tassels;** small amount of black **velvet** for heart; **cinnamon potpourri; lace and gold beads;** two ³/₄-yard-long pieces of narrow **tatting or lace; spray adhesive** and a **hot glue gun and glue.**

For the velvet heart, cut 2 small hearts from velvet. Pin lace to right side of 1 heart piece. Place the 2 heart pieces right sides together and stitch, leaving an opening. Clip seam allowance. Turn heart right side out. Stuff with cinnamon potpourri. Slipstitch opening closed.

For box, apply spray adhesive to wrong side of 1 or 2 doilies and attach to top of box, overlapping edges. Gather together 2 or 3 more doilies into bundles and tack with thread in the center. Glue to box. Tack or glue velvet heart and remaining decorative items to top of box as desired. Glue narrow lace to bottom edge of box top. Place lid on box and mark edge of top. Glue lace or tatting below line on side of box bottom.

Simple Country Folk

1½ cup packed brown sugar

1 cup butter or margarine, softened

1 egg

1 to 2 tablespoons water

3½ cups all-purpose flour

2 teaspoons ground cinnamon

1 teaspoon ground nutmeg

½ teaspoon ground cloves

Lightweight cardboard

Edible Decorator Paint; see page 18

Preheat oven to 350 degrees. In a large mixing bowl, beat together sugar and butter until fluffy. Add egg and water; beat well. In a small bowl, stir together dry ingredients. Add dry ingredients to beaten mixture; stir until well combined.

Using patterns on pages 78 to 79, cut shapes from cardboard. On a floured surface, roll dough out to an ⅛-inch or a ¼-inch thickness. Lay cardboard shapes on dough and cut out cookies with a sharp knife. Place cookies 2 inches apart on an ungreased cookie sheet. Bake for 10 to 12 minutes.

Prepare **Edible Decorator Paint** according to recipe. Paint as shown in photo. Return cookies to oven for 2 or 3 minutes to set paint. Makes 2 dozen cookies.

Simple Country Folk

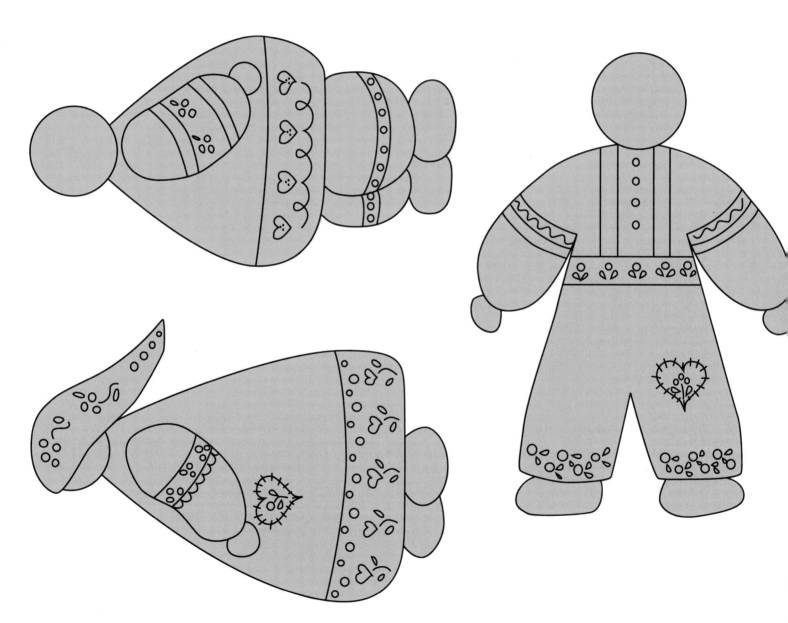

Sweet Sunflowers

1 cup butter or margarine, softened
½ cup sifted powdered sugar
1 teaspoon lemon extract
2 cups all-purpose flour
¼ teaspoon salt
Yellow paste food coloring

1 cup miniature semisweet chocolate
  pieces
½ cup finely chopped nuts

In a large mixing bowl, combine butter, powdered sugar and extract. Add flour and salt; mix until well combined. Add yellow paste food coloring until dough is bright yellow. Cover bowl and refrigerate dough until it is firm enough to shape, about 2 hours.

Preheat oven to 400 degrees. Make 4 to 5 golfball-size balls of dough. Place about 6 inches apart on an ungreased cookie sheet. Flatten the dough with the bottom of a glass. With scraps of dough, make petals for sunflower, molding like clay; see photo for shape. Brush large end of petals with water and attach to the edges of each circle of dough.

Bake for 7 to 10 minutes, removing cookies from the oven before they brown. In a bowl, combine chocolate pieces and nuts. With cookies still on the cookie sheet, sprinkle center of each flower with chocolate mixture, spreading to ¼ inch of flower petals.

Return cookies to oven for 2 minutes to melt chocolate mixture slightly. Cool for 10 minutes on cookie sheet. Remove and cool completely. Makes 4 to 5 large sunflower-shaped cookies.

Hearts Full of Love

1 cup shortening

½ cup sugar

½ cup packed brown sugar

1 egg

3 tablespoons milk

2 teaspoons almond extract

3 cups all-purpose flour

½ teaspoon baking soda

½ teaspoon salt

1 (13-ounce) jar raspberry preserves

Edible Decorator Paint; see page 18

Little Gourmet Clay (optional); see page 134

In large mixing bowl, beat together shortening and sugars. Add egg, milk and extract; beat well. Stir together dry ingredients. Add to mixture; mix well. Cover and chill for 1 hour.

Preheat oven to 350 degrees. On well-floured surface, roll dough to an ⅛-inch thickness. Cut out shapes with large heart-shaped cookie cutter. Place half of the hearts 1 inch apart on ungreased cookie sheet. Spread 1 tablespoon of preserves onto each. If desired, in remaining cookies, cut out hearts with tiny cookie cutter or sharp knife. Set cut-outs aside. Place the tiny hearts on top of the hearts on the cookie sheet. Crimp the edges with a fork or a pastry wheel. Brush underside of cutout hearts with water and place on top of cookies as desired. From scraps of dough cut out small stars, moons and additional hearts. Prepare **Edible Decorator Paint** according to recipe. Use to paint cutouts. Place on cookie sheet. Bake for 7 to 12 minutes, removing smaller cookies if they start to brown. Cool completely.

If desired, add bows. To make bows, prepare **Little Gourmet Clay** according to recipe and color as desired. Roll clay out to an ⅛-inch thickness. Cut clay into strips and form the strips into bows. Makes about 2½ dozen sandwich-style cookies.

Painted Placemat

You will need ½ yard of **muslin**, ⅜ yard of **blue print fabric**, four 1 x 11½-inch strips of **yellow gingham**, **threads** to match, one 12-inch square of **fleece** and blue **embroidery floss**. For the design, you will need 1 **potato**, 1 **manila folder** for the stencil and blue, red, yellow and green **acrylic paints**; see photo. From the muslin, cut one 11-inch-square piece and four 7-inch-square pieces. From the blue print fabric, cut one 12-inch square and 1-inch-wide bias, piecing as needed to equal 50 inches. Cut the potato in half and score a ¼-inch checkerboard grid on the surface. Remove every other section. Dilute the blue paint to an ink-like consistency. Stamp the checkerboard pattern onto the large muslin square. Mark a 4¼-inch-wide circle on each small muslin square. Cut stencils for a tomato and carrot. Mix and dilute the paints to desired colors, including a small amount of green for the tops. Stencil 2 carrots side-by-side onto a circle. Stencil a tomato onto another circle and 2 tomatoes onto a third circle. Cut out each muslin circle, adding ¼-inch seam allowance to all edges. Applique each to checkerboard background, spacing evenly ¾ inch from edge. Decorate edges of small circles with French knots, running stitches and back stitching in blue floss. Stitch gingham strips to edges of checkerboard background, mitering corners. Layer blue-print square, (wrong side up), fleece and design piece (right side up); baste together. Quilt with cream thread; see photo. Sew bias binding onto edges, mitering corners. Fold bias double to back and slipstitch.

Covered Pretzels

Cookie Pretzels

In large mixing bowl, combine butter, ½ cup sugar, 1 whole egg, 1 egg yolk and vanilla until light and fluffy. In a small bowl, sift together dry ingredients. Mix dry ingredients into butter mixture, kneading to a stiff dough. Cover bowl and refrigerate dough for 2 hours.

Preheat oven to 350 degrees. Shape heaping teaspoonfuls of dough into pencil-like strips 6 inches long and ¼ inch thick, by rolling under fingers on floured board. Form into a double twist on greased cookie sheet. Beat egg white with ¼ cup sugar until frothy; brush tops of cookies with this mixture. Bake for 15 minutes. Remove from cookie sheet and cool completely.

Bread Pretzels

In a large bowl, dissolve yeast and 1 teaspoon sugar in warm water, stirring well. Let stand 5 minutes or until bubbly. Add 3½ cups flour, remaining sugar, shortening, egg and salt; beat at low speed of electric mixer until smooth. Stir in enough remaining flour to make a soft dough. Place dough in a greased bowl, turning to grease top. Cover and let rise 1 hour or until doubled in bulk.

Punch dough down and let rest 5 minutes. Turn dough out onto a lightly floured surface and knead 4 to 5 times. Divide dough into 4 equal portions; divide each portion into 4 pieces. Roll each piece into pencil-like strips 6 inches long and ¼ inch thick. Form into a double twist on greased cookie sheet. Beat egg and brush

Cookie Pretzels

- ½ cup butter or margarine, softened
- ½ cup sugar
- 1 whole egg
- 1 egg yolk
- 1 ½ teaspoons vanilla
- 1 ½ cups all-purpose flour
- ½ teaspoon baking soda
- ½ teaspoon salt

- 1 egg white
- ¼ cup sugar

Bread Pretzels

- 1 package dry yeast
- 1 teaspoon sugar
- 2 cups warm water (105 to 115 degrees)
- 6 ½ cups all-purpose flour
- ½ cup sugar
- 3 tablespoons shortening, melted
- 1 egg
- ½ teaspoon salt

- 1 egg

Dipping chocolate

White candy coating pieces

Green candy sprinkles

Multi-colored candy sprinkles

Miniature semisweet chocolate pieces, chopped

Chopped peanuts

Chopped pecans

Chopped almonds

Chocolate sprinkles

Crushed chocolate wafers

Candy-coated fruit-flavored pieces

tops of pretzels. Cover and repeat rising procedure for 50 minutes or until doubled in bulk. Preheat oven to 425 degrees. Bake pretzels for 10 minutes or until golden brown. Place on wire racks to cool.

Melt dipping chocolate in small saucepan. In another pan, melt white candy coating pieces. Dip cookie and bread pretzels as desired. While coating is still warm, decorate with candies or nuts as desired; see photo. Makes 4 dozen pretzels .

Cakes

Little Ladybugs

Easy Chocolate Cake
1 cup water
1 cup butter or margarine
¼ cup unsweetened cocoa
2 cups all-purpose flour
2 cups sugar
2 eggs
½ cup buttermilk or sour cream
1 teaspoon baking soda

Easy Ladybug Frosting
1 cup butter or margarine, softened
2 egg whites
5 cups sifted powdered sugar
2 teaspoons vanilla
Red liquid food coloring
Red and yellow paste food coloring

Large black gumdrops
Small black gumdrops
Black string licorice
Toothpicks

Preheat oven to 375 degrees. Line muffin pans with paper baking cups. In medium saucepan, boil water, butter and cocoa. Remove from heat. In large mixing bowl, mix together flour and sugar. Add cocoa mixture and beat until well combined. Add eggs, buttermilk and baking soda; mix well. Fill each muffin cup half full. Bake for 20 minutes or until inserted toothpick comes out clean. Cool completely.

The cupcake should rise only to the top edge when baked. If the cupcake is not flat on top, trim with sharp knife to make level. Remove baking cups and place cupcakes upside down on plate.

Frost cupcakes with **Easy Ladybug Frosting**, using generous amounts to form the oval shape of a ladybug. For each ladybug, shape a large gumdrop with hands to make head; stick on end of body. Cut tips off of 6 small gumdrops and use for spots on body. Place 1 strip of licorice across center back. Cut 2 pieces of licorice 1 inch in length and attach to the end of a toothpick, then to head. NOTE: To assure the safety of the frosting, which is made with uncooked egg whites, store ladybugs in the refrigerator and eat them within 24 hours. Makes 2 dozen cupcakes.

Easy Ladybug Frosting
Let butter and egg whites come to room temperature. In mixing bowl, combine butter and egg whites and beat well. Gradually add powdered sugar, beating mixture well after each addition. Gently stir in vanilla. Add a few drops red liquid food coloring. Then add red and yellow paste food coloring to make a ladybug color.

Countryside Cottage

Preheat oven to 350 degrees. Grease three 5½ x 3-inch individual loaf pans. In a large bowl, mix together first 6 ingredients. In a large mixing bowl, cream sugar and butter until fluffy. Add honey, eggs and buttermilk; beat well. Fold in flour mixture, beating well. Pour into prepared pans, filling pans ¾ full so that loaves bake with high center peak. Bake for 30 to 35 minutes or until loaves are golden brown. Cool thoroughly before frosting.

Using a straight-edged knife or a decorating spatula, frost each entire ginger loaf with **Ginger Buttercream Frosting**. With a toothpick, trace the outline of the windows and the door on 1 side of each frosted loaf.

Prepare **Easy Chocolate Frosting** according to recipe. Using a decorating bag and a No. 2 writing tip, pipe the inside lattice of the windows with the **Easy Chocolate Frosting**. Changing the same bag to a No. 4 writing tip, pipe window frames and vertical strips for rough-hewn door.

Tint 1 cup of the **Ginger Buttercream Frosting** with yellow, orange and brown paste food coloring until straw colored. Place in decorating bag with either a No. 3 writing tip or a No. 133 tip (which pipes 11 small lines at once). Pipe several layers of vertical lines, starting at peak of each loaf and working down, to resemble thatch. Repeat on other 3 sides of each loaf.

2 cups all-purpose flour

1 teaspoon baking soda

1 teaspoon baking powder

1 teaspoon ground cinnamon

1 teaspoon ground ginger

¼ teaspoon salt

½ cup sugar

6 tablespoons butter or margarine, softened

½ cup honey

2 eggs

½ cup buttermilk

Ginger Buttercream Frosting
7½ cups sifted powdered sugar
1 cup butter or margarine, softened
⅔ cup light cream
1 teaspoon vanilla
½ teaspoon ground ginger

Easy Chocolate Frosting; see page 103

Decorating bag

No. 2 writing tip

No. 3 writing tip or No. 133 special tip

No. 4 writing tip

No. 17 star tip

Yellow, orange, brown, green and pink
  paste food coloring

Tint ½ cup **Ginger Buttercream Frosting** with green paste food coloring. Using a decorating bag with a No. 17 star tip, pipe shrubs at base of cottage and climbing up walls.

Tint small amount of **Ginger Buttercream Frosting** pink or another desired pastel color, and with a No. 17 star tip, pipe a few stars over the green shrubs to resemble blossoms. Dots, made with a No. 2 or 3 writing tip, of yellow or untinted **Ginger Buttercream Frosting** can be placed in the center of the blossoms if desired. Store loaves in refrigerator until serving time. NOTE: To assure the safety of the frosting for these cottages, which is made with uncooked egg yolk, be sure to store the cottages in the refrigerator and eat them within 24 hours. Makes 3 cottage-shaped cookies.

Ginger Buttercream Frosting
Stir together all ingredients in a large mixing bowl. With electric mixer, beat at high speed for 3 to 5 minutes until fluffy.

Luck of the Irish

Preheat oven to 350 degrees. Lightly grease and flour an 8-inch heart-shaped pan. In a large mixing bowl, mix together sugar, oil, milk and eggs. Add dry ingredients; mix well. Stir in poppy seeds, extract and vanilla. Pour into prepared pan. Bake for 50 minutes or until inserted toothpick comes out clean. Remove from oven and cool.

Frost cool cake with **Fluffy Frosting**. Prepare **Little Gourmet Clay** according to recipe. Using a heart-shaped cookie cutter, make shamrocks from clay, scoring down the center of each. Decorate the cake with shamrocks and peach-colored **Little Gourmet Clay** roses. In plastic bag mix coconut with a few drops of purple food coloring; shake well. Use tinted coconut for background and around bottom of cake. Store in the refrigerator until serving time. NOTE: To assure the safety of the frosting for this cake, which is made from slightly cooked egg whites, be sure to store the cake in the refrigerator and eat it all within 24 hours. Makes 12 servings.

Fluffy Frosting
Combine sugar, water and cream of tartar in a heavy saucepan. Cook over medium heat, without stirring, until mixture reaches thread stage (about 230 degrees). Beat egg whites at room temperature until soft peaks form. Continue to beat, slowly adding syrup mixture. Add vanilla and extract, beating well.

2¼ cups sugar

1½ cups cooking oil

1½ cups milk

3 eggs

3 cups all-purpose flour

1½ teaspoons salt

1½ teaspoons baking powder

1½ tablespoons poppy seeds

1½ teaspoons almond extract

1½ teaspoons vanilla

Fluffy Frosting

1 cup sugar

⅓ cup water

¼ teaspoon cream of tartar

2 egg whites

½ teaspoon vanilla

½ teaspoon almond extract

Little Gourmet Clay; see page 134
Peach and green paste food coloring

Grated coconut
Purple liquid food coloring

Crème de la Crème

2 cups water

1 cup butter or margarine

2 cups all-purpose flour

6 eggs

Vanilla Filling

1 small package instant vanilla
  pudding

1 cup cold milk

2 cups chilled whipping cream

1 teaspoon vanilla

Jar of caramel ice-cream topping

Chocolate Leaves and Pinecones

3 or 4 fresh rose leaves

50 small foil-wrapped chocolate eggs
  with foil removed

Small, soft paintbrush

Preheat oven to 400 degrees. In medium saucepan, heat water and butter together to a rolling boil. Reduce heat and stir in flour all at once. Mix for about 1 minute until mixture forms a ball. Remove from heat. Beat in eggs, 1 at a time, beating well after each addition. Drop 3-tablespoon mounds of egg mixture about 3 inches apart on an ungreased cookie sheet. Bake for 20 minutes or until puffed and golden. Remove to wire rack and cool completely.

When cool, cut each puff in half and remove any soft dough inside. Fill with **Vanilla Filling**. Top with caramel topping and **Chocolate Leaves and Pinecones**; see photo. Store in refrigerator. Makes 8 large cream puffs.

Vanilla Filling
In a deep chilled bowl, beat together pudding mix and milk with an electric mixer. Add cream and vanilla to pudding mixture, beating for about 2 minutes until soft peaks form. Cover and store in the refrigerator.

Chocolate Leaves and Pinecones
Wash and dry rose leaves. Melt 10 chocolate eggs in top of double boiler. With paintbrush, paint melted chocolate on back of leaves. Place on waxed paper. Refrigerate until completely set. Carefully peel off chocolate leaves. Refrigerate until ready to use. For pinecones, using a craft knife, cut small slits in the chocolate, starting at the top with 4 small cuts and working toward the base. Work quickly to avoid melting the chocolate. Refrigerate until ready to use. Makes 72 leaves and 40 pinecones.

Ice-Cream Cones

Preheat oven to 350 degrees. Place ice-cream cones in muffin tins. In large mixing bowl, cream butter and gradually add sugar. Beat until fluffy. Add eggs, 1 at a time, beating after each addition. Add dry ingredients to creamed mixture alternately with milk. Stir in vanilla. Fill ice-cream cones half full with batter. (If cones are too full, the cake will rise too much during baking and be difficult to handle.) Bake for 25 minutes or until inserted toothpick comes out clean. Remove cones from muffin tins. Cool completely.

Line muffin tins with paper baking cups and fill half full with remaining batter. Bake for 25 minutes. Cool completely.

Remove liners from cupcakes and frost tops with **Pink Peppermint Frosting**. Turn upside down on cupcake baked in ice-cream cone. Frost cupcake to resemble ice cream using a butter knife. NOTE: To assure the safety of the frosting, which is made from slightly cooked egg whites, be sure to store the ice-cream cones in the refrigerator and eat them within 24 hours. Makes 1 dozen ice-cream-cone cakes.

Pink Peppermint Frosting

Combine sugar, egg whites, and corn syrup in the top of a large double boiler. Add water and beat on low speed of electric mixer for 30 seconds. Place over boiling water. Beat constantly on high speed of electric mixer for about 7 minutes or until stiff peaks form. Remove from heat. Beat 2 minutes or until frosting is thick enough to spread, adding peppermint candy and red food coloring as desired.

12 flat-bottomed ice-cream cones

1½ cups butter or margarine, softened
1½ cups sugar
3 eggs
2¼ cups sifted cake flour
2 teaspoons baking powder
½ teaspoon salt
½ cup plus 3 tablespoons milk
1 teaspoon vanilla

Pink Peppermint Frosting
1½ cups sugar
2 egg whites
1 tablespoon light corn syrup
¼ cup plus 1 tablespoon water
½ cup finely crushed peppermint candy
Red liquid food coloring

Banana Splits

Easy Chocolate Cake; see page 90

White Cake
¾ cup shortening
1½ cups sugar
1½ teaspoons vanilla
2¼ cups all-purpose flour
3 teaspoons baking powder
1 teaspoon salt
1 cup milk
5 egg whites

Cherry Cake
⅔ cup shortening
1½ cups sugar
3 cups sifted cake flour
1 rounded tablespoon baking powder
¾ teaspoon salt
1 cup milk
1 teaspoon almond extract
4 egg whites
½ cup maraschino cherries

6 chocolate cupcakes
6 white cupcakes
6 cherry cupcakes

Prepare **Easy Chocolate Cake** according to recipe.

White Cake
Preheat oven to 375 degrees. Line muffin pans with paper baking cups. In large mixing bowl, cream shortening to soften. Gradually add sugar; cream together until light. Beat on medium speed of electric mixer for 10 minutes, scraping bowl occasionally. Add vanilla; beat well. Combine flour, baking powder and salt. Add dry ingredients and milk alternately to beaten mixture, beating well after each addition. Wash beaters. In a small mixing bowl, beat egg whites until stiff peaks form. Gently fold into mixture. Fill each muffin cup half full with cake batter. Bake for 18 to 20 minutes or until toothpick comes out clean. Cool completely. Makes 2 dozen cupcakes.

Cherry Cake
Preheat oven to 375 degrees. Line muffin pans with paper baking cups. Cream shortening and gradually add sugar, beating well. Combine flour, baking powder and salt. Add dry ingredients and milk alternately to beaten mixture, beating well after each addition. Stir in extract. Beat egg whites at room temperature until stiff peaks form. Fold into cake batter. Add drained and chopped cherries and stir well. Fill each muffin cup half full with batter. Bake for 20 to 25 minutes or until inserted toothpick comes out clean. Cool completely. Makes 2 dozen cupcakes.

Remove liners from 6 of each type of cupcake (all that is needed). Place cupcakes upside down on a plate. Make **Vanilla Frosting** and **Easy Chocolate Frosting**. Frost with matching frosting, placing 1 of each kind in each of 6 banana split dishes. For each banana split, cut a curved end off a Twinkie. Slice in half lengthwise. With frosting on cut ends, stick together to resemble a "banana" and place on a long side of a dish. Repeat, placing second Twinkie on other side of dish. Frost Twinkies with Yellow Frosting, using decorating bag with No. 48 basket weave tip. Drip warmed **Easy Chocolate Frosting** over all. With No. 32 star tip and White Frosting or whipped cream, top each cupcake. Add cherries and walnuts as desired. NOTE: To assure the safety of the frosting, which is made from uncooked egg whites, store banana splits in the refrigerator and eat within 24 hours. Makes 6 banana splits.

Vanilla Frosting

Let egg whites come to room temperature. In a mixing bowl, beat egg whites until stiff peaks form. Add sugar gradually, beating well after each addition. Add vanilla and beat well. Split frosting into 3 portions. Leave 1 divided portion for White frosting. For Pink and Yellow Frostings, add red and yellow food coloring.

Easy Chocolate Frosting

Cream butter in large mixing bowl. Alternating with milk, add sugar gradually, beating mixture well. Add melted chocolate and beat until frosting is well blended.

Vanilla Frosting
3 egg whites
1½ cups sifted powdered sugar
½ teaspoon vanilla
Red liquid food coloring
Yellow liquid food coloring

Easy Chocolate Frosting
¼ cup butter or margarine, softened
3½ cups sifted powdered sugar
3 tablespoons milk
1 ounce unsweetened chocolate, melted

12 Hostess Twinkies or similar cream-filled cakes

Decorating bag
No. 48 basket weave tip
No. 32 star tip
Whipped cream (optional)
Maraschino cherries
Walnut halves

Perfect Parfaits

1¾ cups sugar

⅔ cup butter or margarine, softened

4 eggs

1 teaspoon vanilla

2½ ounces unsweetened chocolate,
  melted and cooled

2½ cups all-purpose flour

1¼ teaspoons baking soda

½ teaspoon salt

1¼ cups ice water

Decorating bag
No. 32 star tip

Cream Cheese Topping
12 ounces non-dairy whipped topping
8 ounces cream cheese, softened
⅔ cup sifted powdered sugar
1 teaspoon vanilla

1 large can cherry pie filling

Multi-colored sugar sprinkles
  (optional)

Preheat oven to 350 degrees. Line muffin tins with paper baking cups. In large mixing bowl, beat together sugar, butter, eggs and vanilla until fluffy. Beat on high speed of electric mixer for 5 minutes, scraping bowl occasionally. Mix in chocolate. Sift together flour, baking soda and salt. Add dry ingredients and ice water alternately to beaten mixture, beating well after each addition. Fill each muffin cup half full with batter. Bake for 30 to 35 minutes or until inserted toothpick comes out clean. Cool completely.

Remove paper cups from cupcakes. For each parfait, cut 1 cupcake in half horizontally and place bottom half in bottom of parfait glass. Using a decorating bag with a No. 32 star tip, add a layer of **Cream Cheese Topping**, then a layer of cherry pie filling. Place top half of cupcake in glass and top with a layer of **Cream Cheese Topping** and then more cherry pie filling. Add a dollop of **Cream Cheese Topping** and sugar sprinkles, if desired. Makes 12 parfaits.

Cream Cheese Topping
In small mixing bowl, mix ingredients together until smooth. Whip mixture until it is stiff and stands in peaks.

Apple Tree See Page 106

1 square=1 inch

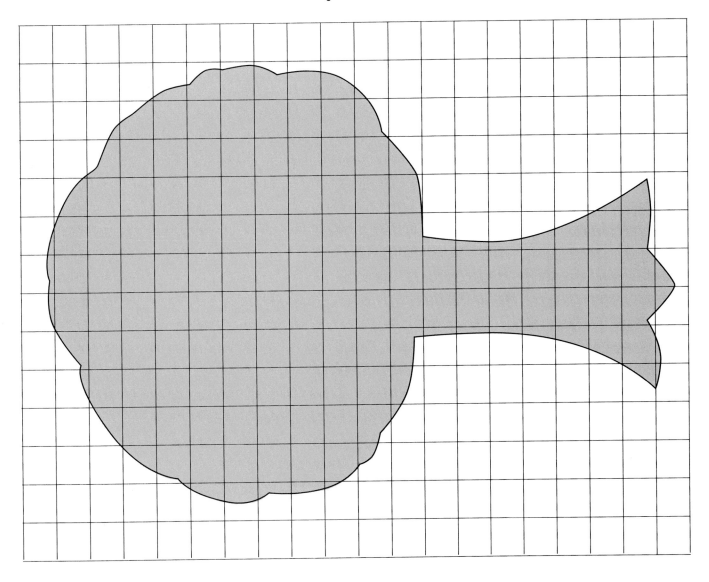

Apple Tree

2 cups sugar

1½ cups cooking oil

3 eggs

2 teaspoons vanilla

2½ cups all-purpose flour

1 teaspoon baking soda

1 teaspoon salt

1 teaspoon ground cinnamon

3 cups peeled diced cooking apples

1 cup chopped pecans (optional)

½ cup all-purpose flour

Lightweight cardboard

Mocha Frosting; see page 108

Preheat oven to 325 degrees. Grease and flour two 13 x 9-inch baking pans. In a large mixing bowl, combine sugar, oil, eggs and vanilla; beat about 1 minute at medium speed. Combine 2½ cups flour, baking soda, salt and cinnamon; gradually add to sugar mixture, beating at low speed of electric mixer until combined. Dredge apples and pecans, if desired, in remaining ½ cup flour; fold into batter. Spoon batter into prepared pans. Bake for 1 hour and 30 minutes or until inserted toothpick comes out clean. Cool in pan for 15 minutes. Remove from pans and cool completely on wire racks.

Using pattern on page 105, cut shapes from cardboard. Using the cardboard shapes, cut cakes, making one cake the trunk and the other the tree top.

With a knife or decorating spatula, cover the tree with green **Mocha Frosting** and the trunk with brown **Mocha Frosting**. Place red wooden apples or cherries on cake as desired. NOTE: Wooden apples are for decoration only; remove before eating cake. Makes 12 to 16 servings.

Mocha Frosting

¾ cup butter or margarine, softened

6 cups sifted powdered sugar

1½ tablespoons unsweetened cocoa

¼ cup plus 1 tablespoon strong coffee

1½ teaspoons vanilla

Green and brown paste food coloring

Decorative wooden apples (optional)

  or maraschino cherries, drained

Mocha Frosting

Cream butter in small mixing bowl. Combine powdered sugar and cocoa; add to butter alternately with coffee and vanilla. Beat until smooth. Divide into 2 portions. Tint 1 portion with brown paste food coloring and the other with green until desired colors are reached; see photo.

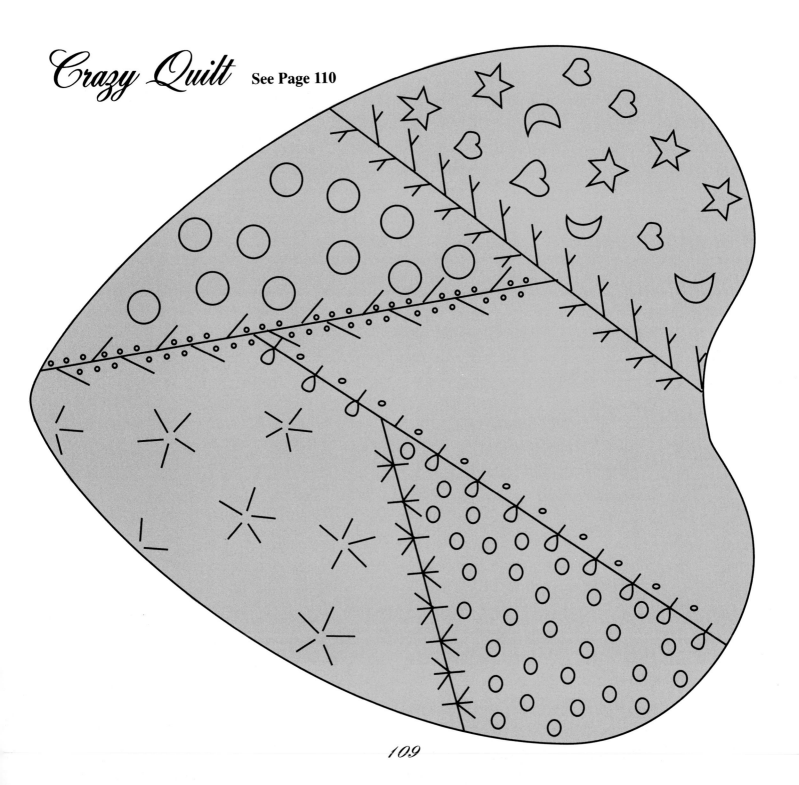

Crazy Quilt   See Page 110

Crazy Quilt

2 cups sugar

1 cup butter or margarine, softened

5 eggs

3 cups sifted all-purpose flour

1 tablespoon baking powder

1¼ cups milk

1 teaspoon vanilla

Basic Frosting

2¼ cups sifted powdered sugar

¾ cup shortening

3 tablespoons milk

¾ teaspoon vanilla

Forest green, blue and rose paste food
  coloring

Decorating bag

No. 3 writing tip

Semisweet chocolate pieces

Decorative silver beads

Flower-decorated hard candies

White candy sprinkles

Preheat oven to 350 degrees. Lightly grease and flour an 8-inch heart-shaped pan. Cream sugar and butter; beat well. Add eggs 1 at a time, beating after each addition. Combine flour and baking powder. Add to creamed mixture alternately with milk. Stir in vanilla. Pour batter into prepared pan. Bake for 25 minutes or until inserted toothpick comes out clean. Cool in pan 10 minutes. Remove and cool completely.

Divide **Basic Frosting** into 3 equal-size portions and 1 small portion. Tint the small portion with forest green paste food coloring, another portion with blue and another with rose. Leave 1 portion untinted. Frost cake according to pattern. Fill decorating bag with forest green frosting. With a No. 3 writing tip, pipe stitches on frosted cake.

Melt enough chocolate pieces to fill an 8-inch round cake pan ¼ inch full. Pour chocolate into cake pan; cool. When chocolate is firm, cut out designs with assorted small cookie cutters. Place shapes on upper rose portion of cake. Decorate 1 white portion with silver beads and the other with flower-decorated candies. Decorate the lower rose portion with white candy sprinkles. NOTE: Silver beads are for decoration only; remove before eating cake. Makes 12 servings.

Basic Frosting

In a mixing bowl, cream powdered sugar and shortening, beating well. Add milk and vanilla, beating until smooth.

Alphabet Blocks

1½ cups boiling water
1 cup rolled oats
½ cup butter or margarine
2 eggs
1 cup sugar
1 cup packed brown sugar
1½ cups all-purpose flour
1 teaspoon ground cloves
1 teaspoon ground nutmeg
1 teaspoon ground cinnamon
1 teaspoon baking soda
1 teaspoon salt
1 teaspoon vanilla

White Frosting
4 cups sifted powdered sugar
¼ cup butter or margarine
¼ cup water
1 teaspoon vanilla
Dash salt

Red Trim Icing
2 cups sifted powdered sugar
Red paste food coloring
Water

Decorating bag
No. 3 writing tip

Preheat oven to 375 degrees. Grease and lightly flour a 13 x 9-inch baking pan. In large mixing bowl, pour boiling water over oats. Add butter and let stand until melted. Add remaining ingredients; mix well.

Pour into prepared pan. Bake for about 30 minutes or until inserted toothpick comes out clean. Cool completely. Freeze cake.

Cut frozen cake into 24 blocks. Warm **White Frosting** and pour over blocks, using a knife dipped in boiling water to smooth imperfections. Using a decorating bag and a No. 3 writing tip, apply **Red Trim Icing** to outline block and make letters. Makes 2 dozen blocks.

White Frosting
Mix all ingredients together in a medium saucepan. Warm over low heat.

Red Trim Icing
In small mixing bowl, combine powdered sugar, paste food coloring and enough water to make a frosting of piping consistency.

Pretty Little Packages

¾ **cup butter or margarine**

¾ **cup sugar**

3 eggs

1½ cups all-purpose flour

½ cup finely ground almonds

1 teaspoon baking powder

Grated rind of 1 orange

2 tablespoons orange juice

Decorators' Buttercream Frosting; see page 70

Red, green and yellow paste food coloring

Decorating bag

No. 47 basket weave tip or No. 3 writing tip

Plastic, silk or Royal Frosting flowers and greenery

Royal Frosting lace

Decorative silver beads

No. 103 rose tip

Preheat oven to 350 degrees. Grease and flour an 8-inch square baking pan. In a medium bowl, cream butter and sugar. Add eggs 1 at a time, beating well after each addition. Add flour, ground almonds, baking powder and orange rind to butter mixture, adding just enough orange juice to make a batter of soft dropping consistency. Spoon into prepared pan. Bake for 1 hour or until inserted toothpick comes out clean.

Cool in the pan for 10 minutes and then remove to a wire rack to cool completely. Cut cake into 4 equal squares. For smaller packages, cut cake into 8 squares.

Prepare **Decorators' Buttercream Frosting** doubling the recipe. Frost cakes. Add real or frosting ribbons. Make frosting ribbons with a No. 47 basket weave tip, using the unribbed side of the tip, or with a No. 3 writing tip. Decorate with plastic, silk or **Royal Frosting** greenery, roses, poinsettias and lilies as desired. Add **Royal Frosting** lace pieces and decorative silver beads, as desired. (See **General Instructions** on pages 164 to 167 for making flowers and lace.)

When making the silver ribboned wreath cake, pipe the ruffled base of the wreath with a No. 103 rose tip. NOTE: Real ribbons, plastic or silk flowers and leaves and silver beads are for decoration only; remove before eating cakes. Makes 8 to 12 servings.

Pumpkin Roll

¾ cup all-purpose flour

2 teaspoons ground cinnamon

1 teaspoon baking powder

1 teaspoon ground ginger

1 teaspoon salt

½ teaspoon ground nutmeg

3 eggs

1 cup sugar

⅔ cup canned pumpkin

1 teaspoon lemon juice

1 cup chopped nuts (optional)

Powdered sugar

Cream Cheese Filling

6 ounces cream cheese, softened

¼ cup butter or margarine, softened

1 teaspoon vanilla

2 cups sifted powdered sugar

Buttercream Frosting; see page 122

Peach, red, brown paste food coloring

Decorating bag

No. 80 or No. 81 special tip

Large marshmallows

Chocolate Leaves and Pinecones; see
   page 98

Preheat oven to 375 degrees. Generously grease a 17 x 12-inch jellyroll pan. Line the bottom of the sheet with waxed paper and lightly flour. In a mixing bowl, sift together first 6 ingredients. In a large mixing bowl, beat eggs for 5 minutes. Gradually add sugar, pumpkin and lemon juice; beat well. Add sifted dry ingredients to mixture; mix well. Pour into prepared pan. Top with chopped nuts. Bake 15 minutes or until inserted toothpick comes out clean.

While the cake is still warm, turn it upside down onto a dish towel sprinkled with powdered sugar. Peel off waxed paper. Roll towel and cake together jellyroll style. Cool.

Unroll cake and remove towel. Spread cake with **Cream Cheese Filling**. Reroll and refrigerate cake.

Prepare **Buttercream Frosting** according to recipe and tint with paste coloring in fall colors for mums. Using a decorating bag and a No. 80 or No. 81 special tip, pipe 1 row of petals at a time, using a marshmallow as the base. Dry on waxed paper. (See **General Instructions** on pages 164 to 167 for making mums.) Prepare **Chocolate Leaves and Pinecones** according to recipe. Arrange mums and **Chocolate Leaves and Pinecones** on pumpkin roll. Refrigerate until ready to use. Makes 12 servings.

Cream Cheese Filling

In medium mixing bowl, cream the cream cheese and butter until fluffy. Add vanilla. Gradually add powdered sugar, mixing until smooth.

Buttercream Butterflies

¾ **cup shortening**

2¼ **cups sifted cake flour**

1 **cup sugar**

1 **teaspoon baking powder**

1 **teaspoon salt**

¾ **teaspoon baking soda**

¾ **teaspoon ground cinnamon**

¾ **teaspoon ground cloves**

1 **cup buttermilk**

¾ **cup packed brown sugar**

3 **eggs**

Lightweight cardboard

Buttercream Frosting; see page 122
Blue, pink and violet paste food
  coloring
Decorating bag
No. 3 writing tip

Black licorice
Black licorice laces

Preheat oven to 350 degrees. Grease and flour two 9-inch round cake pans. In medium mixing bowl, cream shortening. Sift in flour, sugar, baking powder, salt, baking soda and spices. Add buttermilk and brown sugar. Mix until combined; beat vigorously for 2 minutes. Add eggs and beat 2 minutes. Pour batter into prepared pans. Bake for 30 to 35 minutes or until inserted toothpick comes out clean. Cool cakes for 10 minutes. Remove cakes from pans and cool completely on wire rakes.

Using a sharp knife, cut each cake into a 5½-inch circle. Cut each circle in half and place 2 halves together, round sides touching. Using the patterns on pages 120 and 121, cut shapes from cardboard. Cut cakes into butterfly shapes using cardboard patterns.

Prepare **Buttercream Frosting** according to recipe. Divide into 3 portions. Add blue paste food coloring to 1 portion, pink to another and violet to the third. Frost cakes as shown; see photo. Use a decorating bag and No. 3 writing tip to make designs according to pattern. Cut 2 licorice strands 4½ inches long and place on frosted cakes as shown in photo. Cut 4 pieces of licorice lace 2½ inches long and push into top of cakes to form antennae. Makes 8 to 12 servings.

Buttercream Butterflies

Hats Off to the Graduate

½ cup shortening

1 teaspoon vanilla

½ teaspoon salt

1 cup sugar

2 eggs

2 cups all-purpose flour

2½ teaspoons baking powder

¾ cup milk

Buttercream Frosting

7 cups sifted powdered sugar

⅔ cup milk or water

½ cup shortening

½ cup butter or margarine, softened

2 teaspoons vanilla

½ teaspoon salt

12 graham crackers

Pineapple preserves or topping

Red and black shoestring licorice

Preheat oven to 375 degrees. Lightly grease and flour muffin tins. In a large mixing bowl, combine shortening, vanilla and salt. Gradually add sugar; beat until light and fluffy. Add eggs, 1 at a time, beating thoroughly after each addition. In a small bowl, sift together dry ingredients. Add dry ingredients and milk alternately to creamed mixture. Fill prepared muffin tins half full. Bake for 15 to 20 minutes. Remove from pan and cool completely.

Using a generous amount of **Buttercream Frosting**, frost the sides of the cupcakes and place them upside down on a plate. Frost the tops of the graham crackers. Spread a thin layer of pineapple preserves over the tops of the cupcakes. Press a graham cracker on top of each cupcake. Cut a 3-inch piece of licorice for each tassel. With a knife, score the licorice at the point where the tassel will fall across the edge of the cap. Attach to the frosted cracker. Makes 2 dozen.

Buttercream Frosting

In a large mixing bowl, beat all ingredients at low speed with an electric mixer until well combined. Beat at high speed for 2 to 4 minutes until light and fluffy.

Weber High School
Diploma of Graduation
the Class of 19
WEBER

Afternoon Tea

2¼ cups all-purpose flour

1½ cups sugar

⅓ cup unsweetened cocoa

1½ teaspoons baking soda

¾ teaspoon salt

1½ cups water

½ cup cooking oil

1½ tablespoons vinegar

½ teaspoon vanilla

Chocolate Cream Cheese Filling

8 ounces cream cheese, softened

⅓ cup sugar

1 egg

⅛ teaspoon salt

6 ounces semisweet chocolate pieces

4 ½-inch chocolate licorice pieces

Whipped cream

Preheat oven to 375 degrees. Lightly grease and flour muffin tins. In a large mixing bowl, stir together flour, sugar, cocoa, baking soda and salt. Stir in water, oil, vinegar and vanilla; mix until well combined. Fill prepared muffin tins half full.

Drop about 1 tablespoon of **Chocolate Cream Cheese Filling** in the middle of each cupcake. The filling will sink down while baking. Bake for 20 minutes. Cool completely. Remove from tins.

Make a small hole in the side of each cupcake and insert 1 end of a piece of licorice. Bend the licorice to form a handle. Insert the second end. Top each cupcake with a small amount of whipped cream. Makes 2 dozen.

Chocolate Cream Cheese Filling
In a bowl, mix first 4 ingredients until well combined. Stir in chocolate pieces.

Candies

Checkers, Anyone?

16 ounces yellow candy coating pieces

Square candy molds
Small bunny molds

16 ounces pink candy coating pieces

Melt candy coating pieces in double boiler. Pour some of the melted coating into square molds, making 32 squares. Pour some additional candy coating into 12 bunny molds; let the bunnies set and then remove them from the molds. Pour remaining coating into bunny molds and place an already set bunny on top of each new mold, making it two-sided. Cool completely. When bunnies are set, remove from the molds and place in the refrigerator for about 1 hour. Repeat, pouring squares and bunnies with pink candy coating.

Remove bunnies from the refrigerator and clean by scraping off excess candy coating around mold joinings.

Place candy squares, alternating colors, on a square serving dish or cookie sheet. Arrange the pieces to resemble a checkerboard. Place the bunnies on the checkerboard. Makes 64 checkerboard squares and 24 bunnies.

Watermelon Wedges

7½ cups sifted powdered sugar

8 ounces cream cheese, softened

½ teaspoon watermelon-flavored oil
  (optional)

Pink and green paste food coloring

Miniature semisweet chocolate pieces

In a large mixing bowl, stir together powdered sugar, cream cheese and flavoring until completely mixed. Divide mixture in half. Place half in a small bowl and add pink paste food coloring. Mix until well combined. Divide remaining mixture in half again and place into 2 small bowls. Add green paste food coloring to 1 bowl; mix until well combined. Leave remaining mixture white.

Roll the pink candy into a 2½-inch diameter roll; set aside. Take the white candy mixture and roll it out with rolling pin until it is long and wide enough to fit around the pink roll. Place the pink roll onto the flattened white candy and roll the white around the pink. Repeat, rolling and wrapping the green candy around the white and pink roll. Wrap completed roll with plastic wrap and chill for 1 to 2 hours.

Cut roll into slices ¼ inch wide and then cut the circles in half. Cut halves in half again, if desired. Press miniature chocolate pieces upside down into each watermelon slice; see photo. Makes 3 to 4 dozen small watermelon-shaped candies or 1½ to 2 dozen large candies.

Frosty Lace Hearts

Nonstick spray coating
Old-Fashioned Hard Candy; see
   page 146
½ **teaspoon cinnamon- or mint-**
   flavored oil

4 ounces white candy coating pieces
Small, soft paintbrush

Line 2 cookie sheets with foil. With the handle of a spoon, draw 6 heart shapes, 4 inches across, into the foil on each cookie sheet for patterns. Spray with nonstick spray coating. Prepare **Old-Fashioned Hard Candy** according to recipe. After boiling has stopped, stir in desired flavoring.

Using a spoon and holding it close to the foil, drizzle candy in a small line around heart pattern. Continue to drizzle candy side to side, then top to bottom, within the heart shape to achieve lace look. Cool until set.

Melt white candy coating pieces in double boiler. With paintbrush, brush candy coating over cooled hearts. Let set until firm. Carefully peel candy-coated lace hearts from foil. Makes 1 dozen hearts.

FEBRUARY

SUN

Little Gourmet Clay

⅓ cup butter or margarine, melted

⅓ cup light corn syrup

1 teaspoon vanilla

½ teaspoon salt

3¾ cups sifted powdered sugar

Assorted colors of paste food coloring

In large mixing bowl, mix together butter, corn syrup, vanilla and salt. Mix in powdered sugar. Knead until smooth, adding more powdered sugar, if needed, to make clay pliable and not sticky. Divide mixture into portions depending on the number of colors desired. Add desired food coloring to each portion. Knead until color is thoroughly combined.

Shape clay with hands, rolling pin or knife, much as you would molding clay. To attach 2 pieces of clay together, use a toothpick to make cross-hatching pattern on 1 piece; gently press cross-hatched side of 1 piece to another smooth piece.

Apply to frosted or plain cakes, cookies, cupcakes, brownies, graham crackers, candies, gingerbread people or holiday breads. If desired, clay can be decorated with cinnamon candies, semisweet chocolate pieces and other cake decorating trims. NOTE: **Little Gourmet Clay** can be refrigerated in plastic bags for up to 2 weeks. Let stand at room temperature to soften. Makes 1½ cups.

Little Gourmet Clay Roses
Take a tiny ball of clay and roll out. Roll up jellyroll fashion to make center bud. Shape 3 to 4 small petals with hands, curling the edges slightly (Diagram 1). Position petals around center bud and pinch at the bottom to secure them together (Diagram 2). For leaves, take a tiny ball of clay and roll out flat. Using a straight pin, cut out leaf shapes. Draw veins with the pin (Diagram 3). Repeat to make as many roses and leaves as desired. Using dots of icing, attach roses and leaves to the top of cookies or cakes.

Diagram 1

Diagram 2

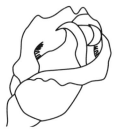

Diagram 3

Horns of Plenty

6 sugar ice-cream cones

Homemade Marzipan
1¾ cups superfine sugar
½ cup water
⅛ teaspoon cream of tartar
1¼ cups ground almonds
1 or 2 drops almond extract
1 large egg white
Sifted powdered sugar

Assorted colors of paste food coloring
Assorted Halloween candies

In a teapot, heat water to boiling. To mold sugar cone, place over teapot spout until pliable. With fingers, turn tip of cone up to resemble cornucopia and hold until set. Push back cone around lip for a roughened look. Allow to dry.

Divide **Homemade Marzipan** into desired number of portions depending on fruits and vegetables desired. Add paste food coloring to each portion and knead until color is evenly distributed. Roll or shape marzipan with hands to make different fruits and vegetables. Use a small amount of brown-tinted marzipan to make stems. Fill sugar-cone cornucopias with marzipan fruits and vegetables and with assorted Halloween candies. Makes 6 cornucopias.

Homemade Marzipan
Cook sugar and water in small saucepan over low heat, stirring occasionally, until sugar is dissolved. Add cream of tartar and quickly bring to a boil. Boil until soft-ball stage (240 degrees). Remove from heat and beat until mixture turns cloudy. Add ground almonds and extract. Whisk egg white lightly and add to the pan. Return to pan to low heat and cook for 2 minutes, stirring constantly. Lightly dust a board or work surface with powdered sugar and turn out the marzipan. Cover with plastic wrap and cool completely. Knead the marzipan for 2 to 3 minutes or until it is completely smooth and free of cracks.

Sundae Best

3 tall sundae glasses

Gumballs, candy pieces in decorative wrappers, gumdrops, jelly beans or wrapped taffy pieces

Hot glue gun
Glue sticks
3 (6-inch) craft foam balls

5 to 6 yards of assorted decorative ribbon
Plastic drinking straws (optional)
Ornamental cherries (optional)

Fill each sundae glass with gumdrops, gumballs, jellybeans or other desired candy. Using glue gun, attach craft foam ball to top of each glass. Glue coordinating wrapped candy to each ball working from bottom to top. Decorate with coordinating ribbon. Glue on straws and cherries as desired; see photo. NOTE: This project is for decorative purposes and should not be eaten. Makes 3 candy sundaes.

China Blue

16 ounces white candy coating pieces

Small, soft paintbrush
12 assorted candy molds

8 ounces blue candy coating pieces
8 ounces green candy coating pieces

Gold thread

Melt half of the white candy coating pieces in double boiler. With small paintbrush, paint areas in candy mold white as desired. If shape is large enough, the white candy coating can be placed in with a spoon. Allow to dry. Melt blue candy coating pieces in double boiler. Pour blue candy coating over the white candy coating already in the mold and allow to harden. When the candy coating is completely set up, remove from molds.

Melt remaining white candy coating in double boiler. Paint white areas of molds as before. Melt green candy coating pieces in double boiler. Pour green candy coating over white candy coating and cool as before.

Heat a needle and make a hole through each candy piece at the top for the hanger. Put gold thread through the hole and tie at top. Makes 2 dozen 2-inch candies.

NOTE: If you do not have 12 candy molds, you may want to make the candy in smaller batches.

Home Sweet Home

Royal Frosting

4 cups sifted powdered sugar

3 tablespoons meringue powder

6 tablespoons water

Pink, blue and yellow paste food
coloring

Box large shredded wheat cereal
squares

2 cups marshmallows

1 tablespoon butter or margarine

Old-Fashioned Hard Candy; see
page 146

Root beer-flavored oil

Cloth leaves

Speckled jelly beans

Large rock candy eggs

Using **Royal Frosting**, make pink roses and small blue drop flowers with yellow centers. (See **General Instructions** on pages 164 to 167 for roses and drop flowers.) Let flowers dry overnight. Store remaining **Royal Frosting** in a grease-free airtight container and refrigerate, saving to attach flowers to nests.

Steam open large cereal squares over boiling water. Gently pull apart the squares, leaving them in long pieces when possible. In a small saucepan, melt marshmallows and butter. Gently mix with the shredded wheat. Shape a third of the mixture over an inverted bowl to help form a nest shape. Cool. Repeat twice more. For small nests, divide mixture into 6 portions.

Prepare **Old-Fashioned Hard Candy** according to the recipe. Add root beer flavoring as desired. With a spoon, drizzle the candy onto waxed paper, making branch-like shapes; see photo. Let set.

Attach flowers, cloth leaves and hard candy branches to nests using **Royal Frosting** as glue. Fill nests with jelly beans or rock candy eggs. Makes 3 large nests or 6 small nests.

Royal Frosting

In a medium mixing bowl, beat all ingredients with an electric mixer for 7 minutes or until stiff peaks form. Tint with desired food coloring. Cover frosting with damp cloth to keep it from forming a crust when exposed to air. Keep tips that are in filled decorating bags tucked into damp paper towels.

Divinity Snowmen

2 cups sugar

½ cup water

½ cup light corn syrup

2 egg whites

½ teaspoon vanilla

Black or chocolate licorice

Little Gourmet Clay; see page 134 or
   orange gumdrops
Orange paste food coloring

Yarn in different colors
8 to 12 small decorative black hats
8 to 12 small decorative brooms

In a medium saucepan, cook sugar, water and corn syrup over medium heat. Bring to a boil, stirring constantly. Cook to light crack stage (265 degrees), stirring occasionally. While sugar mixture is cooking, beat egg whites in a large mixing bowl until stiff peaks form. Add vanilla. When the sugar mixture has finished cooking, pour it slowly over the egg whites, beating constantly. Beat until the divinity starts to loose its gloss and will hold a shape.

With buttered hands and working quickly, shape divinity into balls of 3 graduating sizes. For each snowman, stick a toothpick in the top of 1 of the largest balls and attach middle-sized ball. Then stick another toothpick in the top of the middle-sized ball and attach a small ball for head.

Cut licorice into pieces for eyes, mouth and buttons. Press into divinity where appropriate; see photo. Prepare **Little Gourmet Clay** according to recipe and color with orange paste food coloring. Shape noses or cut gumdrops to resemble noses. Make an indention in the divinity and place noses. Handling several different-colored strands of yarn at once, tie yarn around neck to resemble scarf. Add hat and broom. Makes 8 to 12 snowmen.

Old-Fashioned Hard Candy

Nonstick spray coating
Assorted hard candy molds

2 cups sugar
1 cup water
⅔ cup light corn syrup
½ teaspoon cherry- or lemon-flavored oil
½ teaspoon red or yellow liquid food coloring

Spray molds and a marble surface with nonstick spray coating. Arrange the molds on the marble surface. In a medium saucepan, combine sugar, water and corn syrup. Cook to hard-crack stage (300 degrees). Do not overcook. Remove from heat and let sit for 1 minute.

Add desired flavoring and food coloring; stir well. Pour candy into desired molds. When candy is firm, remove from molds. When completely cool, store candy in plastic bags. Makes 2 dozen star-shaped or 2 bear-shaped and 1 rabbit-shaped candies; see photo.

White Mint Chocolates

Assorted open-top cookie cutters

Nonstick spray coating

8 ounces white candy coating pieces

2 (5-inch) colored candy sticks

For molds, spray 12 cookie cutters and a marble sheet or cookie sheet with nonstick spray coating. Arrange cookie cutters on marble sheet or cookie sheet. In a double boiler, melt white candy coating pieces until smooth. Finely crush 1 candy stick and add to the candy coating. Stir. Pour the melted candy coating mixture into molds. Coarsely crush the other candy stick into small pieces and place on the top of the candy while it is still warm. Cool completely and remove from molds. Makes 2 dozen candies.

Buttermint Tree

3 cups sugar

1 cup hot water

½ cup butter or margarine

1 teaspoon vanilla or peppermint-,
   pina colada- or lemon-flavored oil

Assorted colors of liquid food
   coloring

Light corn syrup

Craft foam cone

Wooden plate

In a medium saucepan, cook sugar, water and butter over high heat, stirring constantly. Cook to firm-ball stage (248 to 249 degrees). Pour the sugar mixture onto a buttered marble slab. Pour vanilla or flavored oil and appropriate food coloring, if desired, onto the sugar mixture. Stretch and fold mixture for about 10 minutes until it loses its gloss. Stretch mixture out to form a long roll ½ inch wide. Cut 1-inch-long mints with knife.

To make the tree, apply corn syrup to bottom of craft foam cone and attach to plate. Place a small amount of syrup in a cup. Working from bottom to top, dip each mint in the syrup and attach to the cone. Place any remaining mints in a small bowl. Makes 1 tree.

Topiary Treats

2 (4 ½-inch) clay pots
Mauve and purple paint
Medium paintbrush
Box plaster of paris
2 corkscrew willow sticks

Homemade Marzipan; see page 136
Assorted colors of paste food coloring
Superfine sugar

1 box toothpicks
2 (3½-inch) craft foam balls

Royal Frosting; see page 142
Violet and green paste food coloring
Decorating bags
No. 32 star tip
No. 67 leaf tip
No. 74 special leaf tip
Royal Frosting drop flowers

Coconut
Green liquid food coloring
Red licorice

Paint clay pots as desired. Allow to dry. Put a small piece of plastic wrap in bottom of pots to cover holes. Prepare plaster of paris and fill clay pots to within ½ inch of top. While plaster is still wet, put a willow stick into each pot and hold until set.

Prepare **Homemade Marzipan** fruits according to recipe. Coat finished fruits with superfine sugar. Insert toothpicks in fruit and attach to 1 craft foam ball, covering completely. Attach ball to 1 of the willow sticks in pots. Attach the second craft foam ball to the second willow stick.

To decorate second craft foam ball, prepare **Royal Frosting** according to recipe. Divide into 3 portions. Tint one smaller portion with yellow paste coloring, and 2 larger portions with violet and green paste coloring. Using decorating bag with a No. 32 star tip and violet frosting, pipe large shells over craft foam ball. In a second decorating bag with a No. 67 leaf tip and green frosting, pipe leaves close to shells. With a No. 74 special leaf tip and violet frosting, pipe stars over the shells, covering completely to resemble lilacs. Attach blue **Royal Frosting** drop flowers with a dot of green frosting. (See **General Instructions** on pages 164 to 167 for **Royal Frosting** drop flowers.)

Place coconut in a plastic bag and add a few drops green liquid food coloring; shake well. Cover plaster of paris in 1 clay pot with tinted coconut, and the other with red licorice. Makes 2 topiary trees.

Santa Suckers

Lightweight cardboard
12 sucker sticks
Nonstick spray coating

Old-Fashioned Hard Candy; see
  page 146
Red liquid food coloring
Liquid whitener

Black string licorice
Small round red cinnamon candies

Light corn syrup
Small, soft paintbrush
Red sugar sprinkles
Coconut

Using pattern below, cut santa shape from cardboard. Line 2 cookie sheets with foil. Using a sucker stick, trace santa shape 6 times on each foil-lined cookie sheet. Spray foil with nonstick spray coating.

Prepare **Old-Fashioned Hard Candy** according to recipe. Add 1 drop of red food coloring and 4 drops of liquid whitener to make candy mixture pink. Let candy cool slightly. Spoon candy onto foil, smoothing it out to follow the santa outline. Press a sucker stick into each santa candy. Cut 2 small pieces from the black licorice and push into each sucker for eyes. Push a cinnamon candy into each sucker for nose. Let cool.

Once suckers are cool, apply corn syrup, like glue, with a paintbrush to the top of each santa head. Add red sugar sprinkles to make hat. Apply more syrup and add coconut to make beard and hat tassel; see photo. Makes 1 dozen santa-shaped suckers.

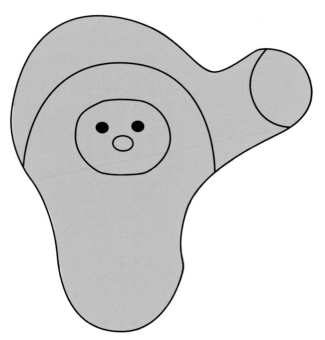

Domino Effect

4 cups sugar

1 (12-ounce) can evaporated milk

½ cup butter or margarine

12 ounces semisweet chocolate pieces

1 (7-ounce) jar marshmallow creme

1 teaspoon vanilla

6 ounces miniature white candy
  coating pieces

In medium saucepan, cook sugar, milk and butter over medium heat. Bring to a boil and boil for exactly 9 minutes. Remove from heat. Add chocolate pieces and stir until dissolved. Add marshmallow creme and vanilla, stir until smooth.

On plastic wrap, roll fudge to a 12 x 4½-inch rectangle, ¼ inch thick. Cut fudge into three 12-inch-long rectangles. Wrap and chill in refrigerator for 2 hours. With a knife, cut each cooled fudge rectangle into 5 pieces. Wipe knife clean after each cut. Make a vertical indention with butter knife in the middle of each rectangle. Allow cut fudge to warm to room temperature.

When soft, push white candy coating pieces upside down into fudge to resemble dominoes; see photo. Makes 15 domino-shaped candies.

Sweet, Sweet Childhood

¼ cup butter or margarine

4 cups miniature marshmallows

6 cups crisp rice cereal

Funnel

Clear and colored plastic wrap

Assorted ribbons

Thin wire

Sugar

Green, red and yellow liquid food
  coloring

3 flat-bottomed ice-cream cones

Light corn syrup (optional)

Marshmallow ice-cream topping

Multi-colored candy sprinkles

In a large saucepan, melt butter over low heat. Add marshmallows and stir until completely melted. Remove from heat. Add cereal; stir until well coated. For kisses, using a buttered spatula, press a sixth of the cereal mixture into buttered funnel. When cereal mixture will hold its shape, remove from funnel. Let set until firm. Repeat twice more.

When rice kisses are set, cover with plastic wrap, placing a short ribbon inside the plastic wrap for each kiss with a few inches of ribbon extended out. Secure wrap by twisting thin wire around plastic wrap, catching ribbon at top of each cereal kiss.

Shape remaining cereal into 3 separate balls. Divide sugar into 3 small bowls. Tint each with liquid food coloring. Roll cereal balls in tinted sugar as desired; see photo. Place balls on top of ice-cream cones. Use light corn syrup to get ball to stick, if necessary.

To serve, pour a small amount of marshmallow topping on each cone and decorate with candy sprinkles. Makes 3 kisses and 3 cones.

Happy Easter

8 ounces blue candy coating pieces

Sheet-type candy egg mold with 2 front and 2 back 3½-inch impressions

8 ounces green candy coating pieces

8 ounces pink candy coating pieces

Nuts, raisins, marshmallows, small candies or gifts (optional)

Decorating bags

No. 2 writing tip

No. 67 leaf tip

Royal Frosting; see page 142

Royal Frosting drop flowers

In a double boiler, melt blue candy coating pieces. Spoon melted candy coating into all 4 molds in the plastic sheet, coating the sides but not filling the molds. Be sure candy coating reaches to the top edges all around to ensure the finished egg will not have gaps on the sides. Chill the filled egg molds in the refrigerator for 5 minutes. Coat inside edges with a second layer of candy coating, again being sure candy reaches to the top edges. Chill another 5 minutes or until firmly set. Remove eggs from molds, turning out onto a folded towel to cushion eggs as they drop. Repeat with green and pink candy coating. Eggs can be filled with nuts, raisins or marshmallows. They can also be filled with candy or small gifts.

After filling the eggs, place a small amount of blue melted candy coating in a decorating bag. With a No. 2 writing tip, pipe a line of candy coating around the edges of 2 blue front egg halves. Align egg pieces, press the blue backs onto the fronts. Remove the tip from the bag and pipe two 2-inch filled circles onto a waxed paper-covered cookie sheet. Press an assembled egg into each candy-coating circle and hold in place for 1 or 2 minutes until the egg and the base are firmly joined. Repeat with green and pink candy coating and egg halves.

Using a decorating bag and candy coating of a contrasting color, pipe borders and leaves; see photo. While borders and leaves are still soft, press on **Royal Frosting** drop flowers as desired. (See **General Instructions** on pages 164 to 167 for **Royal Frosting** drop flowers.) Makes 6 candy eggs.

Rabbit Bench

You will need **pine** in the following sizes: one $\frac{1}{2}$ x 12 x 24-inch piece, one $\frac{1}{4}$ x $\frac{3}{4}$ x 24-inch casing, and one $\frac{1}{2}$ x 1 x 24-inch casing. Also, you will need a **saw**, a **jig saw**, **sandpaper**, **wood glue**, 36 small finishing **nails**, **wood sealer**, white, orange, light green and dark green **acrylic paints**, 1 black fine-tip **permanent marker** and $\frac{3}{4}$ yard of $\frac{3}{8}$-inch-wide blue **grosgrain ribbon**.

Cut 5 back pieces $1\frac{3}{4}$ x $13\frac{1}{2}$ inches long from the $\frac{1}{2}$-inch pine. Using pattern and jig saw, cut top ends of each back piece. Cut a 4 x $10\frac{1}{2}$-inch seat piece from the $\frac{1}{2}$-inch pine. Cut 2 support pieces $10\frac{1}{2}$ inches long from the $\frac{1}{4}$-inch casing. Cut 2 arm pieces $5\frac{1}{2}$ inches long and 2 leg pieces $4\frac{1}{2}$ inches long from the $\frac{1}{2}$-inch casing. Sand all pieces.

Place back pieces on flat surface and mark horizontally $2\frac{3}{4}$ inches and $4\frac{3}{4}$ inches from bottom (unshaped) ends. Place back pieces $\frac{3}{4}$ inch apart with one $10\frac{1}{2}$-inch support above $2\frac{3}{4}$-inch line; glue and nail. Repeat with second $10\frac{1}{2}$-inch support on $4\frac{3}{4}$-inch line.

Place seat piece on lower support; glue and nail securely from back side of bench. Place arm pieces on upper support, aligning edges; glue and nail from back side. From front of bench, put legs in place; glue and nail to seat. With bench upright, nail arms to legs. Coat bench with wood sealer.

Paint seat, arms, legs and supports light green. Wrap masking tape around first, third and fifth back pieces 4 inches below shaped ends. Paint tops dark green. Paint bottoms orange. Paint 2 remaining back pieces white.

Transfer carrot top, carrot stalk and rabbit face patterns to back pieces with pen. Paint orange noses on rabbits. Use finger to paint orange cheeks. Cut ribbon into 2 equal pieces. Tie like necktie and slide over top of wood piece; tighten.

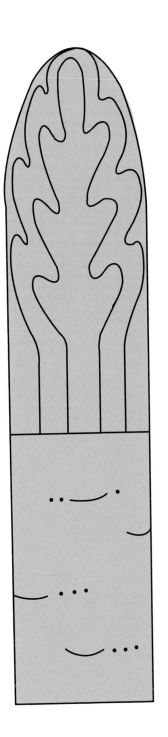

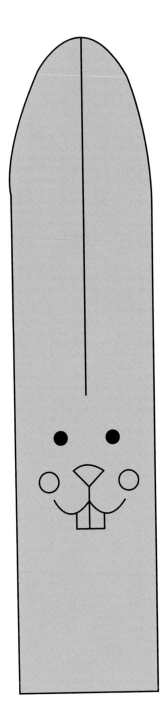

General Instructions

Decorating Bags

Choose decorating bags that are easy to use. Decorating bags made of plastic-coated cloth or a synthetic material are reusable but must be washed and dried each time the frosting color is changed. You'll probably need several. Look for them at department stores and craft shops. If you prefer, you can make disposable decorating cones (see directions, below) from parchment purchased from craft shops. These eliminate cleanup because you can make a different cone for each frosting color and throw them away when you've finished decorating. Use either type when a decorating bag is called for in a project.

Rolled Parchment Cone

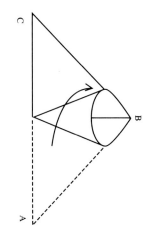

To roll a decorating cone, start with a 17x12x12-inch parchment triangle. Hold it with the long side at the bottom (see diagram). Curl the lower right corner (A) over to point (B) to form a cone. Hold points (A) and (B) together with one hand. Bring corner (C) around the front of the cone so that points (A), (B) and (C) meet and there is no opening at the tip. Fold points down into the cone. With masking tape, secure the outside seam to about 1 inch from the tip. With scissors, snip off ½ to ¾ inch from the tip, depending on the size of the decorating tip being used. Drop the desired decorating tip into the cone so that the top comes through the hole. Using a knife or frosting spatula, half-fill the cone with frosting or filling. Fold in the top corners, then roll the top down to meet the frosting or filling level.

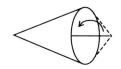

Hand Position

To hold the decorating bag, place the full end in the palm of your writing hand and force the frosting toward the tip by squeezing with the same hand. Use your other hand to guide the tip of the bag. Practice controlling the flow of frosting by regulating the amount of pressure you apply to the decorating bag.

Writing ♥ Lines ♥ Dots

Use a No. 2 or a No. 3 writing tip. To write or make lines, hold the decorating bag at a 45-degree angle to the writing surface. Guiding the tip just above the surface with your free hand, squeeze with your writing hand. To end, gently touch the tip to the surface, release the pressure, then lift off. For dots, hold the decorating bag at a 90-degree angle with the tip almost touching the surface. Squeeze out a dot of frosting. Stop the pressure, then lift off. Uniform pressure will make uniform dots.

Lace Pieces

Use a No. 2 writing tip and **Royal Frosting** only (see recipe, page 142). Copy the pattern on paper as many times as desired, leaving a space between the individual designs. Tape waxed paper over the designs. Press the frosting out, gently tracing around designs. Make many more pieces than required because lacework is fragile and may break easily when handled. Dry pieces for 1 or 2 hours. Pipe an outline on the surface to be decorated and press in the dry lace pieces while the outline frosting is still wet.

Lilies

Use a No. 74 special leaf tip, **Royal Frosting** (see recipe, page 142) only and a lily nail. Press a 2-inch foil square into the lily nail. Pipe a long petal from the center of the foil-covered nail out and over the edge of the lily nail, bringing the petal to a point. Pipe 2 more petals, spacing them to make a 3-pointed star. Pipe 3 more petals in the spaces between the first 3, overlapping slightly. Pipe a green star, with a No. 16 small star tip, deep into the center and push in artificial stamens. Remove the flower, still on the foil, carefully from the lily nail. Dry the flower on the foil overnight. Peel the foil from the flower.

Roses can be made with either a buttercream type of frosting or with Royal Frosting (see recipe, page 142). Refrigerate buttercream roses until chilled before placing them on a cake. Royal Frosting roses should dry overnight at room temperature.

Stars ♥ Rosettes ♥ Shells

Use a No. 16 small star tip, a No. 19 medium star tip or a No. 32 large star tip. For stars, hold the bag at a 90-degree angle with the tip just above the surface to be decorated. Squeeze out frosting, stop the pressure and then lift off. For rosettes, hold the bag and squeeze out the frosting as for the star. Continue to squeeze, moving the tip slightly to the left, then up and around in a clockwise direction until you are back at the starting point. Stop the pressure and pull away. For shells, hold the bag at a 45-degree angle. With the tip just above the surface, squeeze the frosting until a full mound is formed. Ease the pressure and pull the tip down until it touches the surface. Stop the pressure and pull away. Start the next shell at the stopping point of the previous one (shells will overlap slightly).

Roses ♥ Rosebuds ♥ Ruffles

Use a No. 101 small rose tip, a No. 104 medium rose tip or a No. 127 large rose tip. For roses, secure a piece of waxed paper to flower nail with frosting. Pipe the center by touching the tip to the paper, bringing the tip up and turning the nail at the same time to form a cone shape. Keep the tip upright and the thick end of the tip at the base. Pipe a petal around the cone to make a bud, turning the nail while at the same time pressing the bag. To make the surrounding petals, hold the decorating bag at an angle with the narrow end of the tip turned out slightly. Starting halfway up the bud, pipe a row of standing petals, turning the nail counterclockwise while moving the tip up and down in a half-moon arch.

Continue adding petals in the same manner, overlapping the petals as you go. To pipe a rosebud, start with a center cone, then pipe more petals around until the bud is the size desired. Make ruffles with a rose tip by pressing out the frosting in a continuous stroke, moving the tip up and down to create an overlapping pattern.

Drop Flowers

Use a No. 225 small drop flower tip, a No. 131 medium drop flower tip or a No. 190 large drop flower tip. For open petals, squeeze out the frosting, stop the pressure and then lift the tip away. For swirled petals, turn the hand holding the decorating bag as far to the left as possible, press the frosting out gently, then (still pressing) turn the cone to the right as far as possible. Add a dot or dots of frosting in a contrasting color desired, for the center.

Mums

Use a No. 80 or a No. 81 tip. Pipe a circular mound of frosting in the center of a waxed paper square secured to a flower nail. Make the mound the size of the desired flower. Hold down the outer curve of the tip's half-moon opening at a 90-degree angle and press out short ½-inch petals around the mound. Pipe the next row between the petals of the first row, making these slightly shorter and pulling the tips up slightly. Continue until the mound is covered, with each row slightly shorter and more up-tilted.

Poinsettias

Use a No. 74 special leaf tip and **Royal Frosting** only (see recipe, page 142). Secure a square of waxed paper to a flower nail with frosting. Pipe 4 petals about 1⅛ inches long, forming a cross. Add 4 more petals between these. Pipe a second layer of 5 petals about ¾ inch long on top. With a No. 2 writing tip and green frosting, pipe tiny dots in the center for the stamen.

Leaves

Use a No. 65 small leaf tip, a No. 67 medium leaf tip or a No. 69 large leaf tip. With the tip at a 45-degree angle, point it just above the surface to be decorated; squeeze out enough frosting to make the base of the leaf. Continue squeezing, but ease the pressure as you pull away. Stop the pressure, then lift off. For curly leaves, wiggle your hand as you squeeze.

Drop flowers, mums and poinsettias can be made with either a buttercream type of frosting or with Royal Frosting (see recipe, page 142). Buttercream drop flowers should be made right on the cake. Refrigerate all other buttercream flowers until chilled before placing them on a cake. Royal Frosting flowers should dry overnight at room temperature.

Index

–♥–

All of us at Meredith® Press are dedicated to offering you, our customer, the best books we can create. We are particularly concerned that all of the instructions for making the projects and recipes are clear and accurate. We welcome your comments and would like to hear any suggestions you may have. Please address your correspondence to Customer Service Department, Meredith® Press, Meredith Corporation, 150 East 52nd Street, New York, NY 10022, or call 1-800-678-2665.